# A THANKFUL HEART



DAVID A. CHRISTENSEN

CFI
An Imprint of Cedar Fort, Inc.
Springville, Utah

ISBN 13: 978-1-4621-1674-4

Published by CFI, an imprint of Cedar Fort, Inc.
2373 W. 700 S., Springville, UT 84663
Distributed by Cedar Fort, Inc., www.cedarfort.com

LIBRARY OF CONGRESS CATALOGING-IN-PUBLICATION DATA

Christensen, David A., 1949- author.
A thankful heart : 31 teachings to recognize blessings in your life / David A. Christensen.
pages cm
Includes bibliographical references.
ISBN 978-1-4621-1674-4 (perfect bound : alk. paper)
1. Christian life--Mormon authors. 2. Gratitude--Religious aspects--Christianity.
3. Church of Jesus Christ of Latter-day Saints--Doctrines. I. Title.

BX8656.C4938 2015
248.4'89332--dc23

2015016882

Cover design by Shawnda T. Craig

Edited and typeset by Jessica B. Ellingson

Printed in the United States of America

10 9 8 7 6 5 4 3 2 1

Printed on acid-free paper

Praise for

# *A Thankful Heart*

---

"David Christensen returns with his easy-to-use format of 31 important teachings to study and apply to your life. This time, with *A Thankful Heart*, the idea that an attitude of gratitude brings greater happiness into one's life is invaluable. Using Latter-day Saint scriptures and prophet quotes, along with amusing and inspiring personal anecdotes, Christensen proves that the scientific part of being happy is not only related to the amount of faith and spiritual effort we expend, but it also depends on it. Recognizing blessings from Heavenly Father and filling our heart with abundant gratitude is the key to being happy with ourselves and our lives, and this book is essential in making that happen."

—Tara Creel, reviewer at *Deseret News*

# Contents

Introduction.....1
The Beginning.....5
A Key.....9
A Marker.....14
Poor Bookkeepers.....18
Glad to Be Who We Are.....22
Remembering.....27
Highest Advantage.....31
Eventual Exaltation.....36
Cherishing Blessings.....41
So Much Grateful to God.....46
Repentance and Forgiveness Show Gratitude.....50
Greatest of All Sins.....55
How Can We Adequately Thank Him?.....60
Gratitude for the Atonement.....66
Submission and Peace.....71
The Blessings of the Restoration.....76
Thankfulness and Gratitude.....81
His Divine Companionship.....86
Prayers of Gratitude.....91
Abundance.....96

The Test of Our Devotion and Gratitude .......... 100
Thank the Creator .......... 105
Becoming Grateful .......... 109
Enjoy Your Blessings Now .......... 114
Refinement and Stature .......... 119
Blessings in Hardships .......... 123
Happiness .......... 129
Save to Be Saved .......... 134
Daughters of Eve .......... 139
Gratitude for Grace .......... 143
Paint It on Your Heart .......... 147
About the Author .......... 153

# Introduction

Do you know there is a science of gratitude? Studies abound in research and examination to determine how having a sense of gratitude impacts our lives. I decided to comb through a few of the findings and research. I found a pattern in each: having a thankful heart and an attitude of gratitude produces many positive benefits. Among them are results like becoming more socially acceptable, improving health, giving a boost to career and professional aspirations, stabilizing emotions, reducing narcissistic tendencies and self-centeredness, dramatically elevating self-esteem over time, improving relaxation and helping sleep patterns, adding productive longevity to life, increasing energy levels, promoting positive marriage relationships, and even attending to our appearance and how we look to others. The list goes on: deepening friendships, improving management skills, making social networking more productive and fulfilling, increasing productivity, improving decision-making, and reducing the negative impact adversity has on our lives. In my review of a sampling of the scientific data collected about gratitude, I found exactly zero (none, nada, zilch) negative impacts.

Drilling down in the research to find the central benefit of living with a thankful heart and attitude of gratitude, I have found one fundamental answer: happiness. Plain and simple, everything boils down to being happier in our lives.

It is interesting what Joseph Smith taught, "Happiness is the object and design of our existence; and will be the end thereof, if we pursue the path that leads to it; and this path is virtue, uprightness, faithfulness, holiness, and keeping all the commandments of God" (*Teachings of the Prophet Joseph Smith,* selected by Joseph Fielding Smith [Salt Lake City: Deseret Book, 1976], 255–56).

There's something innate in all of us—we want to be happy! Joseph taught that to be happy, virtuous, upright, faithful, and holy, we must keep all the commandments. One of the key commandments He has given us is to receive our blessings "of the Lord, with a thankful heart in all things" (D&C 62:7). Being thankful helps us see God's hand in our lives. It helps us recognize more constantly the role of the Savior and the Atonement. It opens the door for you to feel and recognize promptings from the Holy Ghost.

We see ourselves differently and relate better to our fellowman. We are kinder and more uplifting when we live with gratitude. American playwright and novelist Thornton Wilder described it best when he said, "We can only be said to be alive in those moments when our hearts are conscious of our treasures" (*Our Town*, New York: HarperCollins, 2003).

I once heard someone say that gratitude is not only the greatest of virtues, but the parent of all others. Joseph F. Smith proclaimed: "The grateful man sees so much in the world to be thankful for, and with him the good outweighs the evil. Love overpowers jealousy, and light drives darkness out of his life. Pride destroys our gratitude and sets up selfishness in its place. How much happier we are in the presence of a grateful and loving soul, and how careful we should be to cultivate, through the medium of a prayerful life, a thankful attitude toward God and man" (*Gospel Doctrine*, 5th ed. [Salt Lake City: Deseret Book, 1939], 263).

Gordon B. Hinckley taught, "Absence of gratitude is the mark of the narrow, uneducated mind. It bespeaks a lack of knowledge and the ignorance of self-sufficiency. It expresses itself in ugly egotism and frequently in wanton mischief. . . . Where there is appreciation, there is courtesy, there is concern for the rights and property of others. Without it there is arrogance and evil" (in *Conference Report*, October 1964, 117).

Having a thankful heart helps us to see a bigger picture and gives us a more complete vision of life. It enhances our ability to reframe our challenges and adversities, to see the blessings associated in all things. Plus, it can be contagious. Showing gratitude for others and the experiences of our lives is energizing and gives us strength. Elder Wirthlin noted, "Gratitude turns a meal into a feast and drudgery into delight. It softens our grief and heightens our pleasure. It turns the simple and common into the memorable and transcendent. It forges bonds of love and fosters loyalty and admiration. Living in thanksgiving daily is a habit that will enrich our lives and the lives of those we love. But how do we make this part of who we are?" (Joseph B. Wirthlin, "'Live in Thanksgiving Daily,'" *Ensign*, September 2001).

The Lord simply states, "Thou shalt thank the Lord thy God in all things" (D&C 59:7).

Isn't it interesting that Heavenly Father has given us the main ingredient for our pursuit of happiness—that which He knows His children want the most. To be happy, let's begin with keeping the commandment to be thankful and grateful for all things.

The objective of this book is to suggest ways we can make gratitude a part of our lives and develop a thankful heart. Each chapter begins with a teaching from a latter-day prophet or woman leader in The Church of Jesus Christ of Latter-day Saints. Each quote is followed by a story, commentary by other prophets, or other ideas to invite understanding and application of the principle being taught. You will then be invited to answer a few questions for self-examination and ideas for application. I then share a few scriptures and give you a final thought. Jacob shared my hope for your experience when he said, "Now in this thing we do rejoice; and we labor diligently to engraven these words . . . hoping that our beloved brethren and our children will receive them with *thankful hearts*, and look upon them that they may learn with joy" (Jacob 4:3; emphasis added)

If you like, you may take a chapter a day and seek to apply the principles taught in your daily walk and talk. You will finish in a month. Or you can be more conventional and read it cover to cover at your own pace. Whichever method you choose, I invite you to consider securing a journal to record your feelings. Organize a way to list the things you are most grateful for. One way is to have a section for people you are most grateful for and another list for experiences that enrich your life. Maybe you could list five things each day you are thankful for or perhaps list where you have seen the hand of the Lord in your life on a daily basis. Watch for His divine signatures, fingerprints, and tender mercies, and record them. Maybe you can have a place in your journal for special quotes about thankfulness that inspire you. There are many ideas of how to organize them. While some prefer a digital approach, I suggest that there is something empowering about crystallizing your feelings and thoughts by writing in a journal with pen in hand.

I hope you will enjoy reading this book as much as I have enjoyed studying and writing it.

Happy reading!

# 1
# The Beginning

"A grateful heart is a beginning of greatness. It is an expression of humility. It is a foundation for the development of such virtues as prayer, faith, courage, contentment, happiness, love, and well-being." (James E. Faust, "Gratitude As a Saving Principle," *Ensign*, May 1990)

Recently I visited a trout ranch in Wyoming nestled in the forested slope on the east side of a small range of mountains. It was simply beautiful! There were ten or eleven pristine terraced fishing ponds each separated by small waterfalls cascading down the gentle descent. Each of the ponds was teaming with large trout. It was easy to see large fish swimming and feeding on insects and water bugs. Occasionally a trout spotted a fly or mosquito slightly above the surface of the water. Its white undersides flashed when it visibly jumped above the surface, causing a splash or boiling ripple as it consumed the insect. Farther up the hill several brooding tanks contained thousands of smaller fish. A few tanks had tens of thousands of tiny, newly hatched minnows less than a half-inch long, while others had hundreds of finger-sized fish. Eight or ten tanks each contained larger fish. The owner of the ranch shared with me the workings and systems of raising the prized trout. He pointed out the fishing ponds below and commented how they were used for recreational activities held on the ranch for corporate retreats. He further explained that the hatchery enterprise shipped loads halfway across the state to stock lakes and streams so that anglers could enjoy the universal sport of fishing. Many of these trout would one day be mounted by their catchers, becoming the subject of proverbial growing fish tales told and retold. Other of the stock was sold to restaurants, becoming a chef's delight as tasty fare for hungry customers. I marveled at how much enjoyment, sport, nutrition, and recreation (not to mention financial economy with employment and profits) came from this beautiful spot on the planet.

"Where does the water come from that feeds your tanks and ponds?" I asked. His reply was interesting: "All we do here on the ranch is made possible by a spring that bubbles out of the side of the mountain." He pointed to a place up the hill about a quarter of a mile away. "There is a spring that feeds water to this ranch and runs 365 days a year. Despite subzero temperatures in the winter, the spring never freezes over. It produces a high volume of water per minute right out of the side of the mountain day in and day out."

Think of it. Living water springing forth from the ground less than a quarter of a mile away was the source feeding this cradle of life that impacted wildlife, angler, and connoisseur. It fed the economic interest and the life of the ranch. Take away the spring and everything else goes away. The headwaters created the possibility of bringing so many things to life and doing so much good.

Thus it is with gratitude. Thankful feelings springing forth from our hearts form the headwaters of greatness in our lives. Appreciation multiplies and expands our prayers while giving us more courage to meet the challenges of each day. It makes our prayer life more effective and thus makes our connection with heaven stronger. Being thankful helps us see clearly. It feeds our faith and solidifies our trust in the living God. Living with an attitude of gratitude nourishes our courage and produces a complete trust in Heavenly Father as the Great Giver of all that's good. It brings a critical sense of humility to our lives. It inspires a sense of contentment with what we have, instead of us being challenged with coveting and yearning for the position or trappings of others' success. It replaces gloom, despair, and pessimism with happiness and joy. When we are thankful, we are more charitable and loving. In short, gratitude produces a sense of well-being.

President Faust identified the benefits and blessings of developing a thankful heart. An attitude of gratitude is the beginning or the "living water" of becoming great. It feeds the feelings of the heart in so many other ways. As we begin our study of gratitude, it's time to do a self-check and see where we are so we can chart a course to a greater life.

Grateful living not only expands our faith, but it also sweetens our enjoyment and gives increase to our happiness. Gratitude is the beginning of more contentment. It is surely the wellspring or the beginning of much good.

### Self-Examination for Greater Gratitude

1. How would you rate your own headwaters of greatness? Do you feel grateful most of the time or only occasionally?
2. What would it take to increase your feelings of gratitude and have less concern relative to your deprivations?
3. Identify three things you are most thankful for.

### Scriptures for Consideration and Marking

Enos 1:1
1 Nephi 2:12
1 Thessalonians 5:18
1 Nephi 1:20
Ether 6:5–9
Alma 34:38

### Parting Thought

Our natural-man world seems to be wired with what I call the "psychology of more." We have a tendency, at least in Western culture, to want more, more, more. It has been my observation that when I experience feelings of appreciation for the things with which I've already been blessed, I feel less inclined to want more.

I sense a spirit of contentment, and my prayer life takes on selfless concern rather than begging Heavenly Father for more. I feel happy for how things are turning out and feel a sense of joy for the presence of others in my life. I'm less critical of the actions of others. My trust and faith in my Eternal Father is more implicit. I must confess that my attitude of gratitude doesn't flow 365 days a year like that Wyoming spring that feeds the trout ranch and so much more. Let us work toward helping the wellspring of greatness flow daily. It is the beginning of our renewed quest for greatness.

# 2

# A Key

"My brothers and sisters, do we remember to give thanks for the blessings we receive? Sincerely giving thanks not only helps us recognize our blessings, but it also unlocks the doors of heaven and helps us feel God's love." (Thomas S. Monson, "The Divine Gift of Gratitude," *Ensign*, November 2010)

Let's consider a real life parable. Perhaps you know some who have experienced similar situations as the characters we will use. Let's call our allegorical friends the Jones family. Brother Jones had experienced a season of extraordinary financial, family, and social successes, followed by a cycle of adversity and extreme difficulty. Following their financial glory days of well-being in almost every regard, misfortune struck in every major area of their lives. Health issues and questions concerning the future gnawed at Brother Jones daily. The financial machine, which once provided for their family with excess, was all but destroyed primarily by the collapse of the global economy. Brother and Sister Jones had been philanthropic and generous with their excess, blessing many lives of those less fortunate. Now they were unable to even meet their own needs. In the midst of their temporal crisis, one of their children offended the Holy Ghost and was left on his own, making a series of poor choices and spiraling in a course of self-destruction. All of this caused Brother and Sister Jones heartache, desperation, and wonderment. As their situation became more and more public, they and their children became embarrassed and more conscious of the success and well-being of others. The sin of comparison amplified their failure and enlarged the wounds of their challenges. Eventually they lost their home, their business, and, to a large extent, their self-esteem. Their efforts to rebound from their financial losses found no traction at first, and their season of distress lingered. They kept their testimonies intact, lived according to their covenants, and sought the Lord, but they occasionally wondered if they had lost their connection to heaven. They even wondered, like the friends of Job conjectured, if they were being punished by God for oversight in keeping the commandments.

One Sabbath day in sacrament meeting, the speakers focused on the subject of gratitude, and the congregation sang the hymns "Because I Have Been Given Much" and "Count Your Blessings." The message of the hymns together with the spirit of the meeting penetrated the hearts and souls of Brother and Sister Jones. Their thoughts turned to gratitude, and they began to focus on their many blessings rather than the challenges they'd experienced over the previous two years. As they truly began to count their blessings, they began to think less upon their adversities. They recognized that the balance of blessings to adversities favored the grace of Christ in their lives. They could see clearly how the hand of the Lord had sustained them through their challenges. Closer examination helped them to see that while their challenges had been significant, things could have been much worse. As their thoughts and hearts leaned more toward thankfulness, a key turned and a new door opened. They readily felt the love of Heavenly Father grow in their hearts. Instead of feeling abandoned by heaven, they sensed abiding care and love from the other side of the veil. They knew they were known by Heavenly Father and could see His tender mercies.

Simultaneously, another interesting thing happened. They were more sensitive to those who were experiencing challenges, and their capacity to reach out, nurture, and lift others increased. Their sense of gratitude helped replace embarrassment for their own problems with a sense of humility. It was as though the Master was refining, polishing, and making them useful in His work with His other children.

It became more evident to themselves and others that they were being blessed. While their challenges did not go away immediately, the "changing seats" in life's journey helped them to see things in their world from a new perspective—God's perspective. That change in attitude and view began to change the outcomes in their lives as well. Soon they found that every dimension of their life improved—not in dramatic ways, but in simple inch-by-inch progress. A new source of adequate income through employment was identified and accessed. They found answers to health problems experienced by Brother Jones, and in time their prodigal son returned and found forgiveness through repentance and faith on the Lord Jesus Christ. Greater blessings flowed. It was as though by counting their blessings, their list of tender mercies increased while their once long list of bumps and bruises shrank. The Lord consecrated their adversity for their gain.

Most of us don't have such dramatic and profound challenges as the Jones Family. However, we can get sucked into feeling like heaven has withdrawn and the Lord has abandoned us. During these times, it is unfortunately easy to focus on our challenges and deprivations. We get discouraged, lose hope for better days, and feel like our uncomfortable station in life is permanent. We forget to count our blessings, we lose our awareness of His hand in our lives, and we get depressed.

I once heard a little saying that went something like this, "Two men look from self-same bars; one sees mud, and the other sees stars." I later learned that it originated in Britain by Frederick Langbridge, a clergyman in the late 1800s. It was given in hopes that people in dire circumstances or even in debtors' jails would look out through the bars of their literal or figurative prisons and see good things ahead instead of focusing on their challenges. As we, like Brother and Sister Jones, intentionally focus upon and count our blessings, our grateful hearts turn the key to figurative prison doors and we are free to trust His love and care. We look at our problems as instructive blessings and stepping-stones to a brighter day.

The Greek philosopher Epictetus once said, "He is a wise man who does not grieve for the things which he has not, but rejoices for those which he has" (The Discourses of Epictetus; with the Encheiridion and Fragments, trans. George Long [1888], 429).

## Self-Examination for Greater Gratitude

1. Take a minute and count ten of your many blessings.
2. Have you found tender mercies in the crucible of adversity? Take a moment and write about one of them in your journal or share them with a loved one.
3. Whom do you know who's going through some challenges? How can you lift that person?

## Scriptures for Consideration and Marking

1 Nephi 18:15–16
D&C 59:7, 21
1 Corinthians 9:11
1 Timothy 2:1

## Parting Thought

I use the teaching of President Monson to conclude this lesson. It is instructive. He taught: "We can lift ourselves and others as well when we refuse to remain in the realm of negative thought and cultivate within our hearts an attitude of gratitude. If ingratitude be numbered among the serious sins, then gratitude takes its place among the noblest of virtues. Someone has said that 'gratitude is not only the greatest of virtues, but the parent of all others' " ("The Divine Gift of Gratitude," *Ensign*, November 2010). Let us be thankful. Let us lift ourselves and others by unlocking the doors that will help us to feel His love.

# 3

# A Marker

"Gratitude is a mark of a noble soul and a refined character. We like to be around those who are grateful. They tend to brighten all around them. They make others feel better about themselves. They tend to be more humble, more joyful, more likeable." (Joseph B. Wirthlin, "'Live in Thanksgiving Daily," *Ensign*, September 2001)

I've always been fascinated with the Book of Mormon story of the Amlicites. They were apostate Nephites who joined with the Lamanites. When fighting in hand-to-hand combat, this presented a problem. Prior battles between the Lamanites and the Nephites were easier to execute because the visible distinction of skin color provided an indicator of who was fighting whom. Now these light-skinned apostate Nephites were beside the dark-skinned Lamanites against the forces of the light-skinned Nephites. The problem was obvious. So the Amlicites marked themselves with a red mark on their foreheads as a distinguishing characteristic. This indicated where they placed their allegiance. Mormon writes, "And the Amlicites were distinguished from the Nephites, for they had marked themselves with red in their foreheads after the manner of the Lamanites; nevertheless they had not shorn their heads like unto the Lamanites" (Alma 3:4). They took an action to show others who they were and who they were not. Mormon continued, "Now I would that ye should see that they brought upon themselves the curse; and even so doth every man that is cursed bring upon himself his own condemnation" (Alma 3:19).

Marking ourselves can also be positive. We mark ourselves by the way we dress, with modesty, cleanliness, and refinement. We mark ourselves by the way we talk, with dignified speech, absent of profanity or crudeness. We mark ourselves by where we choose to spend our time, whom we spend it with, what we do, and how long we do it. It is not difficult to recognize full-time servants of the Lord anywhere in the world, whether in Samoa, Rome, Africa, Chile, or Idaho. White shirts, ties, and nametags mark the elders, and modestly dressed young women with nametags mark the sisters. Those marks are a sure indication you are seeing Mormon missionaries. Whether you're in LaVell Edwards Stadium in Provo, Rice Stadium in Salt Lake City, or Ben Hill Griffin Stadium—the Swamp—in Florida on a fall afternoon, it isn't hard to know who is a Cougar, a Ute, or a Gator by what the fans are wearing. Likewise, professional soccer fans, disciples of a particular NBA team, or followers of the Kansas City Royals mark themselves with shirts, hats, armbands, or even face paint to pledge their allegiance. In the clothing industry, certain labels command more respect in some circles. Styles make a statement in others. Many such cultures and persuasions place a mark or place a value upon a person or an institution.

In that context, let's consider one more time Elder Wirthlin's quote: "Gratitude is a mark of a noble soul and a refined character. We like to be around those who are grateful. They tend to brighten all around them. They make others feel better about themselves. They tend to be more humble, more joyful, more likeable."

While contemplating the message of Elder Wirthlin, I have had certain people who I have crossed paths with in life came to my mind. You and I have been with negative people who emulate the characteristics of a Debbie Downer. Perhaps we have even beat the negative drum ourselves at times. But I don't want to dwell there. It is familiar enough.

Let's spend our time considering those who have blessed our lives with seeing the world through grateful eyes and hearts. I think of James, Randy, Jan, and Barbara, with whom I've been a blessed associate. When I am in their presence, I am energized by noticing more of the good in the world than I'd seen before. They speak of beautiful and hopeful things ahead. They highlight the great things that just happened and where they've seen the Lord's hand. They notice something nice to say about the world, the economy, and even what I'm wearing that day. In their words I hear "We have been so blessed" or "This person is such an asset to this company" or "I just love the snow, don't you?" It's not that they're phony or Pollyannaish in their view of life. They're just thankful people who see the good in the world and in quiet but positive ways live with an attitude of gratitude. I love being around them, even for a few minutes, whenever I am able.

Simply and profoundly stated, we mark ourselves as noble souls with refined character when we live with an attitude of gratitude. Being thankful is noticed and felt by others. Expressing gratitude is uplifting to those around us. Expressing heartfelt appreciation is an indication of humility, charity, and other virtues that make us more likable and useful to the Lord. Consider what mark you exhibit. Let's seek to become more lifting by being more grateful.

**Self-Examination for Greater Gratitude**

1. How can you take steps to mark yourself as a more thankful person?
2. What will you do in the next two hours to begin your journey to become more grateful in your walk and talk?
3. What people do you know who exemplify Elder Wirthlin's quote and have marked themselves as such? Perhaps you can start by thanking them with a phone call, an email, or text.

**Scriptures for Consideration and Marking**

Alma 3:4 | Alma 3:19

2 Samuel 22:50
Luke 2:38
Luke 17:16

## Parting Thought

Being a thankful person is an attitude that can be developed. Though some souls come to earth with that virtue, most of us have to develop it. It often requires us to reframe our world or change our view. It may mean we need to change our vision and find ways to remember our blessings before we consider our deficiencies. This can take some work. I attest that it is worth it. Let's begin to be aware of whether or not we are marking ourselves as noble souls of gratitude.

# 4

# Poor Bookkeepers

"Though imperfect, we mortals do good, sometimes much good. But can we keep mortal goodness in perspective? Comparatively, we are so much quicker to return favors and to pay our debts to mortals—and we should be responsive and grateful. But what of Him who gave us mortal life itself, who will erelong give us all immortality, and who proffers to the faithful the greatest gift of all, eternal life? We are poor bookkeepers, indeed!" (Neal A. Maxwell, " 'Answer Me,' " *Ensign*, November 1988, 31)

Though undeserving in many regards, I am privileged to be the father of eight extraordinary children. Six beautiful girls and two handsome boys call me Dad—a blessing I consider to be one of the greatest given to me and my sweetheart. In my view, being a member of our family is a great place to be. We found that with several children, things ran more smoothly in a stable environment with well-defined expectations. However, I do recall that keeping track and maintaining a sense of fairness to all was one element of those years that tried my soul on more than one occasion. The examples are many to show evidence of what I am referring to. Perhaps you may find some familiarity to the same concerns and relate to what I am trying to say.

We had a system that worked pretty well for helping with the dishes after the dinner meal. Each child took a turn. However, as they grew older and became more involved in sports and Church activities, they often needed to trade their assigned turns. That should be an easy exercise to trade a Tuesday night for a Wednesday night, or some other reasonable switch, right? A system of trades and switches seemed to maintain a sense of fairness and control. However, we found that our children were particularly good at keeping track of whatever it was that gave them advantage. We also found that they had a propensity toward amnesia to justify departure from our standard chore list. Once while living in Florida, our fifteen-year-old daughter, overcome by a sense of guilt, confessed to not having done dishes for over ten months. My wife at first was unable to believe that somehow her own accounting was unaware of this subversive action and that she had somehow vindicated this unjust action by our daughter. Keeping track or making sure the chores were balanced was difficult.

Those were great days! In retrospect, a solution to help things may have been to have engaged one of them as a bookkeeper or an accountant to keep track. Yes, those were good days, but I'm glad they're over.

By definition, a bookkeeper is a person who records, accounts for, and tracks financial transactions of a business. A certified public accountant (CPA) is someone who has taken and passed a battery of tests to demonstrate a higher level of proficiency and expertise according to the law. When an accounting firm takes the position of a third party to examine all records, documents, financial controls, and relationships of a company or entity, they then take on the role of auditor. After examination of all records, the third party auditor issues an official statement commenting on the condition of the company's financial statements and the state of the business.

As Elder Maxwell teaches in the quote at the beginning of this chapter, "we are poor bookkeepers, indeed," when in comes to the accounting of the blessings we've received. Our memories are poor when creating any justification for the blessings given us by our Heavenly Father. We are pretty low-level bookkeepers and accountants with our own remembering unless we pause and take on the role of an auditor. Or better yet, it's best if we concede from the beginning that God's gifts to us are innumerable as compared to our measly human efforts to in any way balance the books. The goodness of our Father is so profound that we will never pay Him back. King Benjamin taught, "I say unto you that if ye should serve him who has created you from the beginning, and is preserving you from day to day, by lending you breath, that ye may live and move and do according to your own will, and even supporting you from one moment to another—I say, if ye should serve him with all your whole souls yet ye would be unprofitable servants" (Mosiah 2:21).

We truly are poor bookkeepers! For the most part, we're pretty forgetful at remembering our blessings when we ask for more. We may even slide into an entitlement mindset, thinking that somehow our limited efforts to keep His commandments justify our request for more. Though we are His extraordinary children and are indeed thankful to Him for our blessings, we are in constant need for additional help. We hope He will give us one more blessing even though we've already surpassed our margin of balance. As we attempt to become better auditors of our own accounts, we become more aware that we will never balance the books and will be forever indebted to Him. He only wants us to keep His commandments. Being thankful and mindful of His merciful hand is simply what we have to offer.

**Self-Examination for Greater Gratitude**

1. What steps will you take to become more aware of the multitude of His tender mercies and blessings?
2. Take one percent of your day (which is precisely 14.4 minutes) and identify three blessings that often go uncounted or unintentionally forgotten. Write them down and make a personal commitment to be more aware of them during the coming week.

3. Regarding number two above, tell someone close to you about those blessings. Or stop now for just a moment and say a silent prayer of gratitude to Father in Heaven. Perhaps a prayer and writing a note or telling someone close would be a good start.

### Scriptures for Consideration and Marking

Mosiah 2:21
Luke 16:1–13
1 Chronicles 16:8
2 Nephi 32:9
Matthew 18:21–35

### Parting Thought

Bookkeeping, accounting, and balancing books come with a trap when speaking of being grateful for our blessings. Our delicate human minds truly do have a propensity to forget blessings large and small. I am reminded of another quote by Elder Maxwell when he said, "Mortal mathematics . . . is forever mistaking who and what counts. Even so, we should be more quick to express genuine appreciation. . . . The arithmetic of appreciation is far less practiced and known than the multiplication tables" (*The Neal A. Maxwell Quote Book*, edited by Cory H. Maxwell [Salt Lake City: Bookcraft, 1997], 147). When we take the time to audit our lives for the blessings we have, it becomes obvious that both in quantity and magnitude we are the beneficiaries of a Heavenly Father who wants to bless us. As we look closely, even our adversities and greatest challenges manifest His love and desire to give us experiences that will make us more like Him.

# 5

# *Glad to Be Who We Are*

"No [person] is a more vibrant instrument in the hands of the Lord than a [person] of God who is thrilled to be who she [or he] is." (Sheri Dew, "Stand Tall and Stand Together," *Ensign*, November 2000)

Why is it that at times in almost every life we wish to be someone different than ourselves? It seems more often than not people are not satisfied with their weight, some wishing they were not so skinny, while others go to all lengths to shed unwanted pounds. Some wish they had more facial or body hair, while others are intent on removing any trace of the stuff. Baldness is somehow perceived as something to be abhorred, and too much hair can be culturally stereotyping. We wish we were not so short, or we feel too tall. Many agonize over their teeth or smile, while others focus on the matters of their feet. Many want to erase the wisdom of a wrinkle or two on their faces, while others strive to appear more mature, more shapely, or more robust. Our desire to adorn ourselves with clothing that is stylish, sexy, powerful, trendy, or unique is generally on our minds any time we are in public. Fitness, vitamin supplements, even prescription drugs are touted as things that will make our lives better and more fulfilling.

Billion-dollar industries are created over our discontentment with ourselves. Many people are obsessed with perceived abnormalities and steer toward anything that makes them more acceptable and socially appealing. Marketing strategies and advertising schemes play on our insecurities and perceived deficiencies. Interesting, isn't it?

There is a fine line between seeking to become a better person (more like the Savior) and becoming excessively interested in ourselves. We are commanded to become perfect. We are encouraged by prophets of God to live according to the precepts of the Word of Wisdom, to educate ourselves, and generally to progress to the end that we can love and serve others more effectively. Progression and becoming better is the Lord's way.

Let me be clear. I believe we should take care of our bodies by being attentive to our weight, fitness, and health. I too take vitamin supplements and like to wear stylish but conservative clothing. I naturally want to stop the clock on my aging and liked having more hair on top of my head. However, may I suggest that we all have an enemy to our souls who understands that when we don't like ourselves or our circumstances, he wins. When we obsess over our bodies (something he doesn't have), then something negative happens to our spirits also. This gives him an advantage in his mission to spoil all that's good. He is not only the father of all lies but also the prince of narcissism. He uses our human propensity for self-centeredness to cause a lot of spiritual problems in our lives.

It is discontentment with ourselves and who we are that causes us to become less than what Heavenly Father created us to be. Out of proper balance, wishing we were somebody we aren't figuratively slaps our Creator in the face and says, "I detest your finest and most ennobling creation, man and woman. You made me defective and certainly deficient."

I recall being extraordinarily shy in most public situations in my younger life. My body type in my early teens was spindly, and most would have considered me to be gangly and thin. I remember struggling to do five chin-ups in junior high gym class, well short of the twenty required for an A. The palms of my hands bore large wax-like scars from a burn accident at age one. While we were not poor, I generally felt like I was second class economically amongst many of my peers. I am sorry to say that my report cards were not something I wanted my mother to save and pass on to my children. I was never on the honor roll and was grateful to pass each year. In short, I didn't like myself much, and I didn't make much of a difference in the lives of those around me. I didn't consciously think about it then, but I remember those awkward youth years as feeling deficient.

In spite of those feelings, I am grateful for parents who instilled in me the desire to be morally clean and in good standing with God. Mom and Dad, the primary leaders and teachers in my life, had created the foundation. Over the next several years, even though I never completely lost my shyness, I found that when I was less worried about what others thought of me and more concerned about what I felt and believed in my heart, I did better. Schoolteachers began to be more positive toward me as I became more positive about learning. I became more passionate about serving a mission. The language training mission (now the MTC) in Provo and two special mission presidents inspired my life with trust, confidence, and affirmation.

In short, during this four- or five-year chapter of my life, the foundation that Mother and Father had given me blossomed. That feeling of being broken or deficient was replaced by a sense of peace, destiny, and self-worth. Instead of cowering over self-imposed limitations, I felt absolute delight in being me. While there is still a multitude of ways I need to improve and progress, I feel pleased to be in my skin. Everything in life has changed by the gratitude I feel.

Why do I share this history and context? Because it speaks to the wonderful quote by Sister Sheri Dew at the beginning of this chapter: "No [person] is a more vibrant instrument in the hands of the Lord than a [person] of God who is thrilled to be who she [or he] is."

What's your story? How did the journey in your life expand or discount how you feel about being you? What can you do to take steps in becoming more content with yourself? May we go to work and become "thrilled" to be who we are. Even though there will always be plenty of things to work on and overcome, something good happens when we are glad we are who we are. Certain seasons of life are challenging. Being a young parent trying to provide for and nurture little ones whose diapers must be changed, who quarrel, and who manifest moments of tantrums can be overwhelming. Sometimes the demands of work, a Church calling, or financial commitments invite depression or a desire to shrink. For some of us who are approaching or are well into the sunset years, growing older can be full of days where we long for the yesteryears. Fight the tendency to be discontent with who you are! Don't give Lucifer any ground on this matter. Learn to have a thankful heart for who you are. Be "thrilled" at every age of who you are becoming. Decide now to engage in the process of feeling happy about being you. The Lord then can use us as vibrant instruments in His work around our neighborhoods and communities.

## Self-Examination for Greater Gratitude

1. Are you thankful and even thrilled to be who you are?
2. What would it take to change the things that keep you from being happy with who you are? Would repentance help?
3. Do you know people who are struggling with being who they are? What can you do to help them see their value? What can you say to change their view of who they are?

## Scriptures for Consideration and Marking

2 Corinthians 9:11
Alma 37:46
D&C 98:1
Moroni 10:8–18
Alma 38:2

## Parting Thought

Writing this chapter reminded me of the life-changing and life-enhancing influence others had in shaping my life to a point where I have come to be grateful for who I am. As parents we have a responsibility to form the foundation and infrastructure. However, I'm reminded of the African proverb "It takes a village to raise a child." We can do much to help each other and other people's children by doing and saying things to make others not only content but "thrilled" to be who they are. And we can pray that others will do the same with our children. Grandparents are in a unique position to add value to their grandchildren. May we contemplate and do as moved by the Holy Ghost in this matter.

# 6

# Remembering

"As I would cast my mind over the day, I would see evidence of what God had done for one of us that I had not recognized in the busy moments of the day. As that happened, and it happened often, I realized that trying to remember had allowed God to show me what He had done. More than gratitude began to grow in my heart. Testimony grew. I became ever more certain that our Heavenly Father hears and answers prayers. I felt more gratitude for the softening and refining that come because of the Atonement of the Savior Jesus Christ. And I grew more confident that the Holy Ghost can bring all things to our remembrance—even things we did not notice or pay attention to when they happened." (Henry B. Eyring, "O Remember, Remember, *Ensign*, November 2007)

Have you ever discovered you could do something you didn't know you were capable of doing? I was shy and inarticulate and don't remember of ever voluntarily raising my hand to ask a question in a class or public setting during my boyhood. To readily offer an answer in a discussion was something I seldom did. I remember a day marked by a change in my life with respect to overcoming my shyness. I do not remember the precise subject of discussion. It was in a class taught by Melvin Hammond at Ricks College in Rexburg, Idaho, in the late 1960s. Though listening and thinking about what Brother Hammond was teaching, I was my usual quiet and reserved self. He turned to me and asked, "David, what are your thoughts about that?" I responded upon request by answering with personal thoughts about the subject. After I answered he paused briefly and in a sincere, soft, and convincing way said something like, "I like your insight and thought, David. I've noticed in your written assignments as well that you offer some insightful thinking." That day I was ready to hear that, I guess. I began to think about questions I could ask or comments I could make in discussions before going to Brother Hammond's class. Soon I was doing the same in my other classes. It was the beginning of a new chapter where the cocoon of shyness was replaced with an aura of quiet confidence. While I'm still reserved by nature, I presently feel that I've developed an art of asking questions or offering answers or insights.

Remembering is also an art that must be developed. Arts are learnable skills. Developing the skill of remembering our blessings is easy for those who naturally have thankful hearts, but it still requires conscious effort. Many of us have spiritual ADD and are almost constantly distracted by selfishness or today's needs. It can be challenging to develop the habit of remembering. However, this important art can be developed with practice and review.

We can learn to remember our blessings. Perhaps one of the best motivators to learn the art of recalling God's goodness to us is to consider the benefits as outlined by President Eyring in the quote at the beginning of the chapter. Let's highlight them. First he said, "I would see evidence of what God had done for one of us that I had not recognized in the busy moments of the day." Clearly seeing something that has been blurry or to which we've been blinded is a blessing. President Eyring continues, "I realized that trying to remember had allowed God to show me what He had done." Next he says, "More than gratitude began to grow in my heart. Testimony grew." Remembering will bless us with greater testimony and a knowledge of God's goodness to us. It helps us see His love. Third, "I became ever more certain that our Heavenly Father hears and answers prayers." Being able to know that our prayers are heard and answered brings confidence in our daily living. Fourth, "I felt more gratitude for the softening and refining that come because of the Atonement of the Savior Jesus Christ." Feeling God's grace brings sweetness and expands our capacities. Our burdens are lightened and we are empowered. Understanding just a little of God's grace is one of the greatest benefits of remembering. Fifth, "I grew more confident that the Holy Ghost can bring all things to our remembrance." Wow, the unspeakable blessing to worthy members of the Church is the gift of the Holy Ghost. As He becomes more operational in our lives, He is one of our greatest blessings next to the Atonement.

So how do we develop the capacity to not only recall but to always remember our blessings and from whence they come? Well, unfortunately there's no pill or prescription I know of that can help us develop this art. Only conscious effort to consider and count our blessings can jumpstart the feelings that spawn remembering. When we start to develop an "it's all about me" perspective, stop and remember. Count your blessings. It's during those moments we can turn our thoughts to when we felt, knew, and realized God's hand in our lives. Remember and reflect on times when you served someone in a special way or accepted the heartfelt service of someone. Stop and think upon Christ and His service to you and all mankind.

Developing the art of remembering brings great blessings. Memory is the mother of feeling. To remember is to call up from our memory bank deposits of feelings of past blessings.

### Self-Examination for Greater Gratitude

1. What will you do to become more skillful in the art of remembering?
2. Take some time to expand your list of blessings given you by remembering.
3. What will you do to avoid forgetting?

## Scripture for Consideration and Marking

Mosiah 2:41
Helaman 5:9
Deuteronomy 4:9
Moroni 7:16–17, 19
Helaman 12:1–2, 5
John 14:25–26
D&C 20:77, 79
Alma 37:13

## Parting Thought

It's important to understand the context of President Eyring's quote. In the address he was trying to teach the importance of writing in our journals. In this regard, this chapter echoes that call to action. By writing in our journals, we are given to practice remembering blessings in the short term, for that day or week. I have found that when I crystallize a thought, an idea, or an insight to writing, something almost magical happens. I think President Eyring's quote embodies what that magic looks like.

# 7

# *Highest Advantage*

"When we contemplate what the Lord has done for us in the past, our present surroundings, and our future prospects, what a blest people we are! I have thought sometimes that one of the greatest virtues the Latter-day Saints could possess is gratitude to our Heavenly Father for that which He has bestowed upon us and the path over which He has lead us. It may be that walking along in that path has not always been of the most pleasant character; but we have afterwards discovered that those circumstances which have been very unpleasant have often proved of the highest advantage to us." (Lorenzo Snow, *Teachings of Presidents of the Church: Lorenzo Snow* [Salt Lake City: The Church of Jesus Christ of Latter-day Saints, 2011], 114)

One of the scriptures I've used most often in counseling with ward and stake members or missionaries is 2 Nephi 2:2. Here Lehi is speaking to his son Jacob. His childhood experience began in adversity and included eight long years in some of the toughest times. Food was always in short supply, causing nursing mothers difficulty in providing nourishment for their babies. They were required to eat raw meat much of the time. Desert winds challenged their movement toward a better future. Nights in the desert were often cold and uncomfortable. Though the record is silent on this matter, its presumable that desert insects, snakes, and rodents were pests in the experience of the travelers. Murmuring family members, no doubt lead by Laman and Lemuel, likely tugged at the emotions of everyone in the caravan, who had sacrificed many of the finer things of life back in Jerusalem. In that context, Lehi says to his young son, "Nevertheless,

Jacob, my firstborn in the wilderness, thou knowest the greatness of God; and he shall consecrate thine afflictions for thy gain" (2 Nephi 2:2).

We will all be challenged by tough times. From the day Adam and Eve were expelled from the Garden of Eden, thorns, thistles, and noxious weeds have been a part of the fallen experience. It's the plan. We have to deal with the matter of providing for ourselves and our families. We have to deal with illness, tired muscles, sprained ankles, broken bones, and other physical anomalies. In addition, the emotional strains of dealing with life can be grueling and seemingly never-ending. Even more difficult can be heart-rending situations involving personal rejection from those we love most. Broken hearts ache when closest family members reject the gospel or become completely cold in things once shared. Earth life is full of opposition and adversity.

In the opening quote, Lorenzo Snow was likely referring to the many challenging days in early Church history when the Saints were persecuted and driven from their homes. Those were hard days for newly forged testimonies in Ohio and Missouri when there was loss of property, life, and virtue. The trail spanning from Nauvoo to the Salt Lake Valley is dotted with hundreds, even thousands, of graves. Beginning again in the hostile environment of the West was not an easy task. However, as President Snow stated, "It may be that walking along in that path has not always been of the most pleasant character; but we have afterwards discovered that those circumstances which have been very unpleasant have often proved of the highest advantage to us."

Yes, the good news is that the Lord has promised us He will consecrate our challenges for our gain (2 Nephi 2:22). He told Joseph Smith in Liberty Jail "that all these things shall give thee experience, and shall be for thy good" (D&C 122:7). To consecrate means to make holy or sacred or to sanctify and bless. The unpleasant almost always proves to be the highest advantage when faith in God supersedes faint hearts and trusting in His will takes the front seat.

I recall a simple experience as a young man during those awakening days I referred to in chapter 5. It was early in my sophomore year when I was cut from the school basketball team. I was sitting in the car in front of our home feeling sorry for myself when I looked down on the floorboard and saw a crumpled piece of paper. I unfolded it and found a poem on it. As far as I'm concerned, it was placed in the car by an angel. Its crumpled state required that I pick it up and unravel it for a divine purpose, that I might discover an important truth. It required that I open it at the precise moment when I was emotionally down and feeling rejected. Its message has blessed my life many times over the past fifty years, and I've shared it with others as often as appropriate. It's a poem about trees. I was elated when part of it was shared by President Monson in October general conference 2013. This poem teaches the truth about challenges and adversity. I hope you will enjoy it too and be inspired by it's simple but profound message.

Trees

The tree that never had to fight
For sun and sky and air and light,
But stood out on the open plain
And always got its share of rain,
Never became a forest king
But lived and died a scrubby thing.
The man who never had to toil
To gain and farm his patch of soil,
Who never had to win his share
Of sun and light and sky and air,
Never became a manly man

But lived and died as he began.
Good timber does not grow with ease;
The stronger wind, the stronger trees;
The further sky, the greater length;
The more the storm, the more the strength.
By sun and cold, by rain and snow,
In trees and men good timbers grow.
Where thickest lies the forest growth,
We find the patriarchs of both.
And they hold counsel with the stars
Whose broken branches show the scars
Of many winds and much of strife.
This is the common law of life.
(Douglas Malloch, "Good Timber," in Sterling W. Sill, *Making the Most of Yourself* [Salt Lake City: Bookcraft, 1973), 23)

## Self-Examination for Greater Gratitude

1. Looking back, what experiences have you had that have helped you grow?
2. How has the Lord consecrated your challenges for your growth?
3. Have you written and recorded your feelings, experiences, and testimony in your journal?

## Scriptures for Consideration and Marking

2 Nephi 2:2
D&C 78:19
Psalm 18:49
Mormon 9:31
D&C 122:7

## Parting Thought

Many of our challenges are a by-product of poor choices. How can the Lord bless us in our mistakes or sins? I will share this wonderful teaching by Elder Richard G. Scott: "I know that every difficulty we face in life, even those that come from our own negligence or even transgression, can be turned by the Lord into growth experiences, a virtual ladder upward. I certainly do not recommend transgression as a path to growth. It is painful, difficult, and so totally unnecessary. It is far wiser and so much easier to move forward in righteousness. But through proper repentance, faith in the Lord Jesus Christ, and obedience to His commandments, even the disappointment that comes from transgression can be converted into a return to happiness" (Richard G. Scott, "Finding Joy in Life," *Ensign*, May 1996). It's important to know that Heavenly Father loves us and will consecrate all our adversities—self-inflicted, unplanned, or random as they may be. Trust Him!

# 8

# Eventual Exaltation

"If you will thank the Lord with all your heart every night for all the blessings of that day you will eventually find yourself exalted in the kingdom of God." (Joseph Smith, quoted in Truman G. Madsen, *Joseph Smith the Prophet* [Salt Lake City: Bookcraft, 1989], 104)

I have had a front row seat in observing the making of angels. Though I am sure each will feel uncomfortable when they read or become aware of this writing, I count them angels. I have been blessed to watch special women in my life be shaped by circumstantial service, health conditions, and the challenging vicissitudes of life.

The first angel has been created right before my eyes. Over forty years ago, she and her husband detected that their two-year-old daughter had lost her speech and was manifesting some other abnormal characteristics. They began a journey in search of a solution, which led them to twenty-six doctors over twelve years. They grasped at every hope for a cure, driving hundreds of miles per week for therapy, purchasing expensive equipment, and engaging others in thousands of man-hours of home therapy. There was little, if any, improvement and many difficult days. However, God was shaping an angel—through years of daily bathing, changing diapers, dressing, hand feeding, administering medicines, enrolling in community programs, organizing a family of seven other children around the needs of their sister—for over four decades. Love has deepened and gratitude increased. I have personally watched the unfolding and blooming of the bride who came into my life worthy and wonderful but has become even greater. This angel calls me sweetheart. I thought my best friend and bride was wonderful when I married her, but I have come to see in her daily living a faithful and stalwart angel saint who loves the Lord and trusts in His all-knowing eye. I am so grateful to have witnessed this.

The second angel was shaped by nearly a century of experience. She was taught by parents who loved and trusted God. Her nature through the thick and thin of life was to live gratefully, acknowledging the tender mercies and grace extended by the Father and the Son, as well as living worthy of the ministration of the Holy Ghost. She was born during a time of severe economic challenges. As a youth, she nearly died of rheumatic fever. Over her lifetime there were many chapters of adversity, but she never complained. Rather, she counted her circumstances as purposeful growth and development of those she loved most. The stories of how the Lord shaped her life are far too many to cite in this chapter. As a child, I fell asleep listening to her many experiences laced with testimony and gratitude to God. I've been inspired and bolstered to see the Lord's hand in all things while I slay my own dragons and climb my own mountains. This second angel and witness of the exalting power of gratitude is my mother.

Let's look again at Joseph Smith's words from the start of this chapter: "If you will thank the Lord with all your heart, every night, for all the blessings of that day; you will eventually find yourself exalted in the kingdom of God."

What is it about those who live with an attitude of gratitude that merits such a profound and distinct pronouncement from a prophet of God? What happens to us when we are genuinely grateful? How is our nature changed and shaped by a mindset that includes the Lord's love and care for us in all things? How does habitual and intentional appreciation each day qualify a person for exaltation? Could it be that thankful hearts are formed and fortified when we submit ourselves to His will, knowing that all things carry His fingerprints? Who can be ungrateful to a Father who promises that even our mistakes, misjudgments, and sins can be consecrated for our gain when we place Him and His Son first in our lives? A heart that constantly expresses and acknowledges the Lord and His mission to give each of us immortality and eternal life approaches purification and readiness to receive all the Father intends to give us.

If living with gratitude has the potential to exalt us, then we can be sure that Lucifer will seek to spoil it and take us in the opposite direction. Let's look at the antithesis of thanking the Lord with all our hearts every day. What is the result of being thankless toward God while thinking everything we are and have comes from our own ingenuity and industriousness? How does the Lord feel toward those who take the credit themselves and do not acknowledge Him and His love toward us? Joseph F. Smith taught, "One of the greatest sins of which the inhabitants of the earth are guilty today is the sin of ingratitude, the want of acknowledgment, on their part, of God and his right to govern and control. We see a man raised up with extraordinary gifts, or with great intelligence, and he is instrumental in developing some great principle. He and the world ascribe this great genius and wisdom to himself. He attributes his success to his own energies, labor and mental capacity. He does not acknowledge the hand of God in anything connected with his success, but ignores him altogether and takes the honor to himself. . . . Now, I read in the revelations through Joseph Smith, the prophet, that because of this, God is not pleased with the inhabitants of the earth but is angry with them because they will not acknowledge his hand in all things" (*Gospel Doctrine*, 5th ed. [Salt Lake City: Deseret Book, 1939], 270–71).

The opposite of having a thankful heart is possessing an attitude of self-centeredness. What is it about thanking the Lord with all our heart on a consistent basis that transforms us to a state worthy of exaltation? Perhaps it chips away at our natural-man tendencies to be selfish. Is it possible that an attitude of gratitude chokes and starves self-centeredness? Maybe instead of feeding the "all about me" perspective, it develops humility when we form the daily, constant habit of acknowledging a loving Father, whose only interest and goal in our lives is our growth. Could it have something to do with manifesting faith, patience, and obedience? Is it because giving thanks establishes a connection with heaven, which produces a love for Him and charity toward our fellow man? Does the thankful heart detain or even extinguish the destructive fire of the universal sin of pride?

Developing a thankful heart is part of acquiring the attributes of godliness. I'm thankful for these two angels in my life who have been extraordinary visual evidences of the exalting power of gratitude in the face of adversity. I hope to learn to be like them, for they truly live by the Savior's example, who said, "Not my will, but thine, be done" (Luke 22:42) while always manifesting a thankful heart.

## Self-Examination for Greater Gratitude

1. How have you learned to be more thankful and less self-centered? Write about it in your journal.
2. Who in your life has been an angel example of one who lives with an attitude of gratitude? Have you told them and expressed gratitude for their example?
3. What is the difference between habitual and intentional gratitude? How will you improve both in your life?

## Scriptures for Consideration and Marking

Psalm 50:14
Revelation 11:17
D&C 59:15
Psalm 136:1
Ephesians 1:16

## Parting Thought

Let us seek to be more grateful. May we learn to recognize the exalting power in true and heartfelt testimony that God loves and knows us and that His only desire is to develop in us the characteristics that make us worthy to have all that He has. Let us close this chapter as we began it. "If you will thank the Lord with all your heart, every night, for all the blessings of that day; you will eventually find yourself exalted in the kingdom of God."

# 9

# Cherishing Blessings

"Hold fast to the blessings which God has provided for you. Yours is not the task to gain them, they are here; yours is the part of cherishing them." (J. Reuben Clark Jr., *Church News*, 14 June 1969, 2: quoted in James E. Faust, "Gratitude As a Saving Principle," *Ensign,* December 1996, 2)

Some time ago, a close friend related to me an experience that I found interesting. He and his friend decided to engage in a serious hike into the Grand Canyon. They planned, prepared, and made reservations with the park service to execute the journey from Northern Utah into Arizona. My friend offered to drive his car. After several hours in the car, they arrived at the trail head, put on their boots and gear, and began the hike into the canyon. After reaching the destination, they made preparations for spending the night at their designated campsite. It was then they realized a major problem. In their enthusiasm to get on the trail, they had left their food in the car. My friend was embarrassed, and while both were mutually at fault, the experienced partner murmured and expressed his dismay about expending so much energy in making the one-way trip into the canyon. By park service design, which required permits, there were a limited number of hikers within close proximity. It looked like they would go to bed hungry and have limited energy for the climb out of the canyon the following morning. My friend indicated that as the darkness of night was settling on the canyon, he paused, expressed gratitude alone for their safe arrival, and then prayed for help. Meanwhile his partner was paralyzed by negativity and self-concern. They both understood this matter was not life threatening, but it certainly had the potential to take the joy out of their journey.

After uttering a silent prayer, my friend determined to go find water at nearby waterfalls. While there, he encountered a few other hikers. They engaged in friendly discussion, and my friend mentioned their situation. His new friends responded with offers to share some of their food. They returned to their campsite, he shared half of the food with his hiking partner, and they went to sleep replenished after all. The next day they enjoyed the beauty of the canyon. They eventually hiked back to their car and began the several-hour drive back home. The experience of the hike became a point of discussion as they traveled. At one point in the discussion, the issue of leaving the food in the car surfaced. My friend expressed his gratitude for how the Lord had answered his prayer to find food. His traveling companion saw it differently and scoffed, rejecting that it had anything to do with God.

A few days later, knowing about the planned hiking trip, I inquired about how it went. He responded about how beautiful it was and shared the blessing of his answered prayer for food. But then he said, "The one real damper on the whole experience is in realizing that [his hiking partner] failed to say thank you even once." He added, "I offered to take my car, which I was happy to do. We started with a full tank and filled up twice. I bought him a meal en route and was led by the Lord to good people in the bottom of the canyon who shared their food with us, allowing us not to go to bed hungry." And then with a little frustration in his voice, he concluded, "In two and a half days with him, he never said thank you for anything. Not once. The only thing he ever talked about was his exploits, his discomforts, and his concerns." He expressed, "I didn't do anything expecting to be thanked. But I confess, I don't think I ever want to do it again."

I know God and Christ are perfect and They love us perfectly. But I am sure They notice whether or not we acknowledge blessings in whatever form they come. Timothy Dexter once said, "An ungrateful man is like a hog under a tree eating acorns, but never looking up to see where they come from" (Timothy Dexter, *The New Dictionary of Thoughts* [Garden City, NY: Standard Book, 1961], 308).

Think again on the quote by President Clark: "Hold fast to the blessings which God has provided for you. Yours is not the task to gain them, they are here; yours is the part of cherishing them." Holding fast to blessings is not difficult. Cherishing blessings is another thing. The dictionary definition of *cherish* is "to love, worship, and adore." Its Latin root refers to "have more charity" (*Oxford American Writer's Thesaurus* [Oxford University Press, 2012]), which is scripturally defined as "kind, and envieth not, and is not puffed up, seeketh not her own," and is even "the pure love of Christ" (Moroni 7:45, 47). I have no doubt that in a remote place in the bottom of a canyon, the food two hungry hikers received that night were a blessing from heaven. But only one of them looked up to see where it came from. The other apparently considered it only a coincidental change in fortune and did not regard it worthy of expressing gratitude to heaven or to his traveling companion.

Jesus Himself shared with us His perspective about ingratitude when He told the parable of ten lepers who had been healed, but only one turned back and gave thanks for the miracle. Luke writes,

> It came to pass, as [Jesus] went to Jerusalem, that he passed through the midst of Samaria and Galilee. And as he entered into a certain village, there met him ten men that were lepers, which stood afar off: and they lifted up their voices, and said, Jesus, Master, have mercy on us. And when he saw them, he said unto them, Go shew yourselves unto the priests. And it

> came to pass, that, as they went, they were cleansed. And one of them, when he saw that he was healed, turned back, and with a loud voice glorified God, and fell down on his face at his feet, giving him thanks: and he was a Samaritan. And Jesus answering said, Were there not ten cleansed? but where are the nine? There are not found that returned to give glory to God, save this stranger." (Luke 17:11–18)

I'm always edified by heartfelt voices who never miss a chance to say thank you. There is something special about people who say, "Thank you for your service," "I appreciate your patience," "Thank you for remembering," "I appreciate your preparation and insight for that lesson," or "We are grateful for you and your time." An expression of thanks lifts and brings warmth to both the giver and the receiver. It has a way of cleansing the wounds sustained in the battles of life. It also helps us see more clearly while maintaining a healthy sense of humility.

### Self-Examination for Greater Gratitude

1. Have you ever later remembered that you forgot to say thank you to someone you should have thanked? Have you fixed it? Today would be a good time to write them a note or give them a phone call.
2. If you've ever felt slighted by another person who forgot to cherish an act of kindness or a gift from you, have you determined to forgive the oversight?
3. How can you remember to be more grateful?

### Scriptures for Consideration and Marking

Moroni 7:45–48
Luke 17:12–19
Psalm 100:4
1 Corinthians 13:1–13
Mosiah 8:19

## Parting Thought

The percentage of lepers who failed to express gratitude to Christ for cleansing their living death is chilling. Surely four or five others were thankful too. I'm betting all of them likely realized at some time that the changing of their wretched lives as lepers was a blessing from God. I want to believe that. It must have been a liberating moment to have this progressive, infectious disease (which causes disfiguring skin sores, painful nerve damage, and muscle weakness) gone, to realize they would no longer be shunned and considered social outcasts. But one sad fact remains. The excitement of the moment caused them to forget the higher and more noble thing to do—have a thankful heart and express appreciation for that life-changing moment. May we have the presence of mind to remember in our life-changing moments, great or small.

# 10

# So Much Grateful to God

"Still in our day, God's power and love are manifest in the lives of His children. I have seen it recently in the lives of faith-filled Saints in Zimbabwe and Botswana. In a fast and testimony meeting in a small branch, I was humbled and inspired by testimonies shared by many—children, youth, and adults alike. Each conveyed a powerful expression of faith in the Lord Jesus Christ. With challenges and difficult circumstances surrounding them, they live each day by putting their trust in God. They acknowledge his hand in their lives and often express it with the phrase 'I am so much grateful to God.'" (Jean A. Stevens, "Fear Not; I Am with Thee," *Ensign*, May 2014.)

Once while I was serving as bishop, a young mother of four moved into our ward. She informed me that her husband had recently been killed in a Scouting-related activity, and she was in the dawn of a new chapter of her life—raising her children without the help of a loving husband. Her life was and is inspiring to me for many reasons. She was as devoted and faithful as anyone I have ever known. My wife and I both agree that she was angel. Her life was a sweet sermon of everything I hope to become someday. Her faith, compassion, and incredible sense of charity were hallmarks to her life. She exhibited a smile, never said a harsh word, and was always about the business of living as the Savior taught. On one particular Sunday shortly after she moved into the ward, she approached me after church and asked if she could talk to me. Within the privacy of the bishop's office, she reached into her handbag, took out a cashier's check with a donation slip, and handed it to me. For a recently widowed woman with four children to raise, the amount of the check was significant. She said, "Bishop, I want to pay my fast offerings and thought it well to talk to you about it." Looking first at the check and then directly into her eyes, I said, "Sister, you don't need to do this. I'm sure with your circumstances you can use at least some of this for important considerations in your life." She looked back into my eyes and said, "Bishop, the Lord has been so good to me! After all the insurance proceeds came after the death of my husband, I met with a financial professional. We've planned for the education of my children in addition to what my husband had earlier planned. We have no debt, and while we will have to be careful, we will be just fine." With some emotion, she leaned over and quietly said, "Bishop, I know there are others who have greater needs than mine. It is my honor and blessing to share my blessings with them through these fast-offering funds. It is an expression of my gratitude to Heavenly Father for blessing us."

Over the years I have spent nearly 15 percent of my life in parts of the world where the people are generally very poor by North American standards. I have observed wonderful people in Mexico, Central America, Chile, the Bahamas, Egypt, and Africa who have so little of the economic blessings we've come to take for granted. I've had the privilege of associating with members, investigators, children in orphanages, and those disenfranchised in senior care centers in these foreign countries. I've also marveled at how happy and content they seem in their circumstances. Generally their commentary about their circumstances included a statement of gratitude that communicated, "I am so much grateful to God."

I recall the image of when one of our sons returned from his mission in South America, he stood in front of an opened refrigerator, gazing upon the contents and saying, "We sure have a lot of food." Another daughter said at the conclusion of her mission, "We have so many options." We have come to take for granted our many options and refrigerators full of leftovers that are often thrown out because we don't eat them before the mold starts its feasting. I remember someone once saying something like, "Every age on the face of the earth has had its challenges and cross to bear. For the pioneers it was making it across the plains and starting anew. For some it was the epidemics of polio, measles, small pox, or black plague. For yet others it was the results of war. Perhaps our greatest challenge is our abundance. We have so much that we forget to thank Heavenly Father for it." It would be well for us to remember, as the African Saints, to be "so much grateful to God."

President Uchtdorf wrote in his December 2014 First Presidency Message of a family in need at Christmas time:

It doesn't take expensive gifts to make Christmas meaningful. I am reminded of a story told by Elder Glen L. Rudd, who served as a member of the Seventy from 1987 to 1992. One day before Christmas a number of years ago, while he was managing a bishops' storehouse, he learned from an ecclesiastical leader about a needy family that had recently moved to the city. When he went to visit their small apartment, he discovered a young single mother with four children under age 10.

The family's needs were so great that the mother could not buy treats or presents for her children that Christmas—she couldn't even afford a tree. Brother Rudd talked with the family and learned that the three little girls would love a doll or a stuffed animal. When he asked the six-year-old son what he wanted, the hungry little boy replied, "I would like a bowl of oatmeal." (Dieter F. Uchtdorf, "Fill the World with Christ's Love," *Ensign*, December 2014)

When the family received the Christmas gifts and the boy his requested bowl of oatmeal, there was no doubt a feeling from both receivers and givers of "we are so much grateful to God." May we become more thankful and feel to say daily, "I am so much grateful to God for His many blessings."

## Self-Examination for Greater Gratitude

1. Have you grown less and less grateful for any of your blessings?
2. Have you told your family, friends, or others how grateful you are for specific blessings?
3. When everything seems to be going well for you (or not going well for you) what can you do to stop and remember how good the Lord has been to you and yours? Make a plan.

## Scriptures for Consideration and Marking

1 Chronicles 16:34
Ephesians 5:20
2 Nephi 9:52
Ezra 3:11
Alma 26:8

## Parting Thought

A wise man once said, "The hardest arithmetic to master is that which enables you to count your blessings" (Eric Hoffer, *Reflections on the Human Condition* [New York: Harper & Row, 1973], 94). It's true! Learning to count and remember our blessings is a big challenge. Elder Neal A. Maxwell said, "Mortal mathematics . . . is forever mistaking who and what counts. The arithmetic of appreciation is far less practiced than multiplication tables" (*The Neal A Maxwell Quote Book* edited by Cory H. Maxwell [Salt Lake City: Bookcraft, 2001], 147). May it be our goal to master the arithmetic of counting our blessings large and small and being "so much grateful to God."

# 11

# Repentance and Forgiveness Show Gratitude

"Our willingness to repent shows our gratitude for God's gift and for the Savior's love and sacrifice on our behalf. Commandments and priesthood covenants provide a test of faith, obedience, and love for God and Jesus Christ, but even more importantly, they offer an opportunity to experience love from God and to receive a full measure of joy both in this life and in the life to come." (Dieter F. Uchtdorf, "A Matter of a Few Degrees," *Ensign*, May 2008)

Early in John's life, he made an important decision: he would never break the law of chastity by having sexual relations of any kind. During his youth he remained true to that commitment. He was a talented athlete in his high school, and parties and after-game activities presented potentially compromising situations. But firm in his commitment, he avoided any situation for possibly encountering temptations that would challenge that personal covenant. He prepared for his mission with a desire to serve the Lord clean and unblemished by sexual sin.

It was not long after he returned from that he met a wonderful girl. When he was in her presence not only did he feel the chemistry of physical attraction, but most important, he wanted to be the best and most worthy priesthood holder he could be. To John, she was beautiful. He could see that she was kind and sensitive, loved children, loved the Lord, and cherished general conference and counsel by living prophets. As he got to know her, his like for her turned into something sweet and deep. He felt she was the person he was going to marry. Finally, John concluded he would ask her to marry him in the near future.

One day he was walking with some new friends from California and discovered they had grown up in the same town his girlfriend had lived. During their discussion, he learned she had a season of her life when she had made some unwise choices, and apparently she wasn't as diligent as he had been in keeping the law of chastity and living the word of wisdom.

Everything had seemed to be so perfect. Now John felt his heart struggle. He wished he'd never learned the disheartening news, but he felt it was important he found out. John postponed his plans to ask her to marry him until he could sort through his feelings.

He attended the temple, fasted, prayed, and read the scriptures. While studying the book of Alma, he read something he had read many times before about the conversion of Alma the Younger: "And it came to pass that as I was thus racked with torment, while I was harrowed up by the memory of my many sins" (Alma 36:17). As John read and then reread that part of the scripture, he realized he was holding his girlfriend hostage by the memory of her sins. He read on, "Behold, I remembered also to have heard my father prophesy unto the people concerning the coming of one Jesus Christ, a Son of God, to atone for the sins of the world. Now, as my mind caught hold upon this thought, I cried within my heart: O Jesus, thou Son of God, have mercy on me, who am in the gall of bitterness, and am encircled about by the everlasting chains of death" (Alma 36:17–18). John turned his thoughts toward the Savior.

The words of the Lord came to his mind, and he quickly looked up the scripture: "Remember the worth of souls is great in the sight of God; for, behold, the Lord your Redeemer suffered death in the flesh; wherefore he suffered the pain of all men, that all men might repent and come unto him. And he hath risen again from the dead, that he might bring all men unto him, on conditions of repentance. And how great is his joy in the soul that repenteth!" (D&C 18:10–13).

An almost audible voice seemed to whisper, "He who has repented of his sins, the same is forgiven, and I, the Lord, remember them no more" (D&C 58:42). At first, John felt ashamed for his judgment and that he had forgotten a doctrine so fundamental to the gospel. And then a rush of peace came over him. His own sins, which seemed to be less serious and of minimal consequence, came into his mind. He knew he also needed the Savior. The girl he was in love with was new, reborn, and near perfect. He knew rebirth had occurred in his heart as well. John felt calm and peaceful.

Ultimately, our lives can be healed only through the Atonement. All of us are sinners and can be made clean through repentance. One of the greatest things we can ever do to show our gratitude to Heavenly Father and our Savior Jesus Christ is to repent and allow the Atonement and the grace of Christ to have full sway in our lives—as well as in the lives of others who repent and are forgiven.

President Joseph Fielding Smith noted,

> One of the greatest sins, both in magnitude and extent . . . is the sin of ingratitude. When we violate a commandment, no matter how small and insignificant we may think it to be, we show our ingratitude to our Redeemer. It is impossible for us to comprehend the extent of his suffering when he carried the burden of the sins of the whole world, a punishment so severe that we are informed that blood came from the pores of his body, and this was before he was taken to the cross. . . . If we really understood and could feel even to a small degree, the love and gracious willingness on the part

> of Jesus Christ to suffer for our sins we would be willing to repent of all our transgressions and serve him. (Joseph Fielding Smith, *Restoration of All Things* [Salt Lake City: Deseret Book, 1945], 199)

Anytime we hold other repentant souls hostage for past misdeeds and transgressions by withholding forgiveness, we show ingratitude (one of the greatest sins) for God's gift to all of us to change and become new again. Let us show our gratitude by repenting of our wrongdoings and allow others the same blessing by forgiving them, as the Savior requires of us. In these ways we more completely live with thankful hearts.

## Self-Examination for Greater Gratitude

1. As you scan your present state of being, how can you express your gratitude to Father in Heaven by repenting? Where will you start?
2. Is there anyone for whom you hold an unhealthy grudge who has sought to be forgiven? If they have not sought to be forgiven, will you take the first step and lay the matter at the Savior's feet, allowing Him to be judge in the matter?
3. Who do you know that might benefit from reviewing President Uchtdorf's counsel? Share it with them.

## Scriptures for Consideration and Marking

Alma 36:16–20
D&C 58:42
D&C 64:34–35
D&C 18:10–13
Mosiah 26:39
Matthew 18:21–22

## Parting Thought

The Atonement of the Savior is the greatest event in history. President Gordon B. Hinckley reminded us, "No other act in all of human history compares with it. Nothing that has ever happened can match it. Totally unselfish and with unbounded love for all mankind, it became an unparalleled act of mercy for the whole human race" (Gordon B. Hinckley, "At the Summit of the Ages," *Ensign*, November 1999). May we examine our hearts and show our love and gratitude by repenting of our sins. Further, may we allow the same to others by forgiving. Anything else is prideful and selfish.

# 12

# Greatest of All Sins

"One of the greatest sins of which the inhabitants of the earth are guilty today is the sin of ingratitude, the want of acknowledgment, on their part, of God and his right to govern and control. We see a man raised up with extraordinary gifts, or with great intelligence, and he is instrumental in developing some great principle. He and the world ascribe this great genius and wisdom to himself. He attributes his success to his own energies, labor and mental capacity. He does not acknowledge the hand of God in anything connected with his success, but ignores him altogether and takes the honor to himself." (Joseph F. Smith, *Gospel Doctrine*, 5th ed. [Salt Lake City: Deseret Book, 1939], 270–71)

It is easy to note, even in a cursory study, that the Lord and His servants have had much to say about the seriousness of not having a thankful heart. For example, Brigham Young taught, "I do not know of any, excepting the unpardonable sin, that is greater than the sin of ingratitude" (*Teachings of Presidents of the Church: Brigham Young* [Salt Lake City: The Church of Jesus Christ of Latter-day Saints, 1997), 177). That's a statement to be taken seriously. The Lord Himself witnessed, "And in nothing doth man offend God, or against none is his wrath kindled, save those who confess not his hand in all things, and obey not his commandments" (D&C 59:21).

There is a significant tendency in society to applaud ourselves in our intellectual, social, and material advancements. We tend to say we've done something quite remarkable. As individuals we have the propensity to give honor to ourselves by inviting others to look at what we have done. We find it easy to pad our résumés with impressive achievements and overinflate self-assessments of our capacities and judgments. In short, we can be inclined to take personal or collective credit for all the good that is done.

Rather than devoting this chapter to the evils of not being grateful, let's consider the blessings and inspiration that come from of having a thankful heart. I would like to share a perspective the Lord has blessed me with during recent years. Let me say first that I have spent a good share of my life in the for-profit sector as well as in academia. Until a few years ago, I had never had any real time in the non-profit arena. I was invited to administer the operations and development of a non-profit entity that provides education to future and returned missionaries, along with others who are seeking to become self-reliant. Those benefiting from this endeavor are individuals in Central America. The organization depends on the consecrated donations of individual benefactors. I am so thankful for my association with wonderful people who have taught me so much about kindness, humility, and anonymous sharing. The experience has been an inspiring one.

The experience has less to do with the amount donated but is more about the characteristics exhibited by thankful hearts. I have watched young married couples struggle on their newlywed resources and entry-level salaries. I've observed others on student budgets. One young priesthood holder and patriarch of his family said, "Brother Christensen, we were moved by Elder Holland's general conference address ("Are We Not All Beggars?" *Ensign*, November 2014) and also an *Ensign* article written by Elder Robert Gay ("Your Journey of Giving," *Ensign*, September 2014). We don't want to be overzealous or unwise, but we feel we've been so blessed. We pay our tithing, and we try to be as generous as we are able in our offerings. But my wife and I feel inclined to do a little more. One way we can acknowledge Heavenly Father's goodness is to share! We have food to eat and a roof over our heads, we manage to save for our future, and we have been blessed with employment. We have two beautiful and healthy small children. I could go on and on. Can we donate ten dollars a month to help someone in Central America have a chance at receiving even a part of those same blessings?" I note that this attitude is not reserved to just a few.

On the other end of the spectrum, I have seen men and women who have been blessed with extraordinary wealth demonstrate the same generous hearts and write checks with five and six figures, while requesting either complete or limited anonymity. They express feelings like, "We are grateful for the Lord's blessings in our financial life. We are compelled to do all we can to bless our fellowman in whatever way we can." Many add comments like, "Heavenly Father is responsible for every penny we have. For whatever reason, He's prospered our choices and hard work, but in the end, all we have is His. Nothing is ours. He's just given us the chance to be stewards of His resources. We hope to be blessed with His wisdom in sharing it properly."

I have had occasion to be with those not of our faith who express similar feelings. I was on an airplane with two gentlemen affiliated with two different Christian denominations who partner in giving to the poor. One of the two philanthropists, in our discussion of a potential project, commented, "Giving to those less fortunate keeps us grounded in remembering that all things come from God. My success is meant to glorify God and bless others. Whatever I have means nothing if I keep it only for myself."

I have noticed that so many of those who give generously according to their circumstances, in a spirit of gratitude, are generally quiet in their approach and without fanfare. Their appreciation and acknowledgment of God is genuine and full of humility. One widow I knew, after acknowledging the goodness of God in her life, simply added the perspective, "I am grateful for my blessings, and while I don't have a lot, I have enough. Paying my tithing is a privilege that has never been negotiable no matter what. Giving to other Church funds and charities is equally an honor. I have more and to spare. How can I not share with others?"

It's true that in many the great discoveries in science, the arts, and the material advancements of the age, the world says, "We've done it!" Individuals often give no credit to God. May we not be guilty of the same. All blessing come from Heavenly Father, who loves us.

## Self-Examination for Greater Gratitude

1. Do you have a testimony of the blessing and privilege of paying your tithes and offerings? Is there someone with whom you should share that testimony?
2. Have you checked your motives lately? Why or why not do you share your gifts?
3. Can you see the Lord's hand in your successes? Are you quick to remember Him and acknowledge His goodness?

## Scriptures for Consideration and Marking

D&C 59:21
2 Timothy 3:1–4
Hosea 11:7
Matthew 18:21–35
Alma 38:14
Mosiah 2:19

## Parting Thought

I will part with the words of Lloyd P. George, who spoke about the seriousness of possessing an attitude of ingratitude while seeking to take credit unto ourselves. He said, "I presume most of us have not thought of that as a serious sin. There is a great tendency for us in our prayers—in our pleadings with the Lord—to ask for additional blessings. Sometimes, I feel, we need to devote more of our prayers to expressions of gratitude and thanksgiving for blessings already received. Of course, we need the daily blessings of the Lord. But if we sin in the matter of prayer, I think it is in our lack of expressing thanksgiving for daily blessings. God is not pleased with the inhabitants of the earth but is angry with them because they will not acknowledge his hand in all things" (Lloyd P. George, "Gratitude," *Ensign*, May 1994). Let us be more grateful in our prayer life.

13

# How Can We Adequately Thank Him?

---

"Gratefully we acknowledge the infinite mind of our Maker, and gratefully ought to offer our tithes and offerings, and earnestly consistent service, in thanks for all that God has given, and keep his commandments in remembrance of the love and providence and purpose of the Creator, the God and Father of us all. . . . Thank God for all this: for life and what sustains it, for loved ones that make it meaningful, for faith and purpose and continuance, always and forever. Thank God for all of this—and much, much more." (Richard L. Evans, "Thanks: for the Organization and Operation of the Earth," *Improvement Era,* February 1968; quoted in Marion G. Romney, "Gratitude and Thanksgiving," *Ensign*, November 1982)

---

One of my personal heroes gave me permission to share his story. Rob Parkinson relates from his personal journal:

> During the holiday season of 2009, my family and I knew this was our last Christmas together. The thirty-year battle was about to end. I started suffering from the symptoms of ulcerative colitis while on my mission in Brazil. When I was thirty-five, the doctors removed my large intestine and told me that I had a related liver disease, primary sclerosing cholangitis (PSC). My only option was a liver transplant. There is no known cure for PSC. The doctors told us my liver would last from one to fifteen years.
>
> This Christmas marked fifteen years from that diagnosis. I was sick, weak, itching, and constantly fatigued. The symptoms of a failing liver were manifesting themselves

more and more. We had tried everything: listing at three transplant centers, evaluating family members as live donors, and promoting organ donation however we could. Because of the nature of my disease, I just didn't move up on the transplant waiting list. This Christmas, as a family, we accepted that the Lord's will was for me to continue my mission on the other side of the veil. It was a tender holiday season as we celebrated the birth of our Savior.

Less than a month later, on Friday, January 22, 2010, I was at my office. I received a phone call from my wife, Tracey. "Did you hear about Jeremy Rose?" she inquired. I had not. Jeremy and his wife, Kristene, had been in our ward when I served as bishop a few years earlier. Jeremy worked construction and was usually out of town on projects. This time his company was working on a project in Hawaii. On Thursday, he fell from a beam, two stories high. His life was in jeopardy and his outlook was uncertain. They put him on life support until his family could travel from Idaho to Hawaii.

Tracey immediately contacted Cathy Hanna, a close friend to Kristene, to ask about Jeremy's situation. They discussed the accident, Kristene's feelings, my situation, and the awkwardness of starting a conversation with the Rose family at a time like this. Cathy wanted to help. She contacted a cousin who contacted her dad, an uncle, who contacted his sister, Hazel, Jeremy's mother. By now, Hazel and Kristene were in Hawaii. The "Gift of Life" transplant coordinator had already visited with them, but they hadn't given much thought to organ donation. They were grieving at the loss of their husband and son.

After receiving the phone call from her brother, Hazel approached Kristene. "I need to tell you about a phone call I received from my brother." Hazel asked Kristene if she knew

Rob Parkinson. Kristene nodded that she did. Hazel then proceeded to tell Kristene about my situation and Tracey's inquiry. More serious thoughts and conversations about organ donation ensued. Seconds turned to minutes, and then minutes turned to hours. Kristene spent time by Jeremy's bedside wondering what to do. After praying, pondering, discussing, and praying some more, Kristene felt that Jeremy wanted her to proceed. She let the transplant team know that she had decided to donate Jeremy's organs but specifically requested that Rob Parkinson receive the liver. As they sat down, Kristene laid her head on Hazel's shoulder and asked if they could pray together. They prayed for my well-being.

When my family received the news, a series of phone calls began. So much had to be coordinated in such little time. Rules had to be broken to get the liver from Hawaii to Salt Lake City, across regional boundaries. Miracle after miracle occurred and our fifteen years of worry and preparation were resolved in one weekend. After eleven hours of surgery, the transplant was a success.

The clock in the hospital room read 11:07. Where was I? What happened? Then I realized. The transplant worked. I was alive. My body felt strangely different. I could tell that a functioning liver was in place. I couldn't move, but I knew that my body now had the ability to heal itself. My whole being felt refreshed. Gratitude overcame me, and I began to cry.

Tracey and my son, Tyce, were at my bedside. I couldn't talk because of the tubes in my mouth and throat. I asked for a paper and a pencil. I simply wrote, "I love you," and we hugged. Then I wrote a note to the Rose family. I asked Tracey and Tyce to make sure Kristene received it.

Since that time, I have thought a lot about gratitude. I

promised myself that I would count my "bonus days." Every day, I wake up and recognize that this is a day that I would not be having if it were not for the Rose family and the miracles performed by the Lord.

How do you thank someone for a gift like that? How do you thank someone for the gift of life? How do you thank someone for even one extra day, let alone thousands of extra days? How do you thank someone for the restoration of health and strength and vim and vigor? How do you thank someone for the ability to laugh and play, to worship and feel His spirit, and to work and face challenges? How do you thank someone for a second chance at life? How do you thank someone for thinking of your need when they are experiencing such shock and grief themselves? How do you thank someone for the opportunity to see missionary sons go and come? How do you thank someone when you hold a new grandchild for the first time? How do you thank someone when you wake up each morning and realize you are home with your wife and family? How do you thank someone when you go for a walk, or see nature's beauty, or hug someone, or converse with a child? Please, how do you appropriately thank? It seems impossible.

I once asked that question of a health care worker in Wisconsin. She told me, "You thank by living your life the best that you can, by trying to be kind to everyone, even the lady in front of you at the grocery store. You thank by constantly expressing your gratitude."

I have learned much from the Rose family and from their Christlike, selfless act of kindness to me and my family. They continually express that they miss Jeremy but that seeing me helps their hearts to heal. That thought brings me joy.

Their selfless act has taught me more deeply about the ultimate selfless act performed by our Savior. He is the

One who thought of us when His own personal suffering was unbearable. He is the One who truly gives us a second chance. He is the One who gives us the gift of eternal life. He is the One who provides our strength. And what does He ask of us? That we live our lives the best that we can, that we follow Him, that we keep His commandments, and that we constantly express our gratitude. Kristene made a plaque that is in our home. It reads, "Gratitude. We choose to celebrate life. Each day is a gift."

How do you adequately thank someone who has saved your life? How can you ever repay someone who has given you another chance? You can't! There's simply not any way in the human capacity to say or show complete and total gratitude for such action. But we can attempt to do so by our actions.

We can show our gratitude by seeking to keep His commandments, which are created to protect and keep us on a course that will make us happy. We can make and keep covenants, which are requirements to receive from Him all that He has, even to have eternal life, which is a god life. This seems so lopsided. We do as He has asked and He gives us more—hardly an exercise in fair play. But it is His economy. He desires to bless us and seems to look for every opportunity within His divine plan of happiness to give us more than we can ever give Him. (Used with permission of Robert G. Parkinson, Rexburg, Idaho)

## Self-Examination for Greater Gratitude

1. Which two or three commandments will you focus on to demonstrate your gratitude for the multitude of His many blessings?
2. Whom can you seek to treat kindly as a way of showing your gratitude for the blessings of how Heavenly Father has treated you?

3. With whom will you teach or share the concepts contained in this chapter that will bless their lives?

## Scriptures for Consideration and Marking

| | |
|---|---|
| Psalm 119:156 | James 1:11 |
| 1 Nephi 8:8 | 1 Nephi 1:10 |
| D&C 14:7 | Mosiah 2:12–14, 34 |

## Parting Thought

The only thing we really have to give the Lord is our desires. He has given us everything and only asks us to give Him our hearts, desires, and will. We can give Him money in tithes and offerings. Do we pay reluctantly? Do we serve and love others only out of duty? We can go to our church meetings, not use tobacco, and complete a Church calling, but do we do it without feeling or in a rote fashion. Until we give Him our heart and desires, we fall short of exhibiting the spark of Him within each of His children.

# 14
# Gratitude for the Atonement

"Gratitude is also the foundation upon which repentance is built. The Atonement brought mercy through repentance to balance justice. How thankful I am for the doctrine of repentance. Repentance is essential to salvation. We are mortal—we are not perfect—we will make mistakes. When we make mistakes and do not repent, we suffer." (Robert D. Hales, "Gratitude for the Goodness of God," *Ensign*, May 1992)

Living in Rexburg, Idaho, and being a member of the faculty at BYU–Idaho, I remember the day when an announcement was made of a new major facility to be built on campus. It was to be a gathering place where students would unite weekly for devotionals, where large numbers of people could unite together and be culturally and spiritually lifted. This wonderful facility came to be known as the BYU–I Center. The announcing statement included that construction would begin immediately and that it would be built on a design-build basis—designed and built simultaneously.

I guess my expectation was that the following week we would see a bulldozer moving dirt, the foundation laid, and a building rise up right before our eyes in a short time. It was a short time later when civil engineers were on the proposed site identifying lines that would become the footprint for the building. There was early activity of large dirt movers and some occasional blasting that shook the ground and let us all know a structure was in process. However, the most curious thing was that the foundation phase took so long. I did not keep a log nor count the days, but looking back, it was easy to see that the foundation creation of a building the magnitude of the BYU–Idaho Center was a long-term phase. In fact, it seems it took over half the total time of building that massive edifice. Creating a foundation is a most critical step in developing a visible structure. It required lengthy and focused development.

So it is with creation of true and lasting change through faith in the Lord Jesus Christ and repentance in His name. It takes time to develop a foundation and infrastructure in the soul before it is ready to receive and understand the grace that is extended to us through the Atonement. That foundation is a profound thankfulness for the unconditional love and willingness of Christ to forgive us, having already suffered for us as sinners.

In my role as a priesthood leader, I have encountered many who feel that after confession of their sins, righteous desires, and a few weeks of a better prayer life, they have repented and are categorically forgiven for serious sin. I found joy with them in their new lighter feelings but felt to teach them that the relief that comes through beginning down the road of repentance is not all that the Lord requires. In my experience, it takes time to create a foundation of profound gratitude, which prepares the heart to receive the total peace associated with complete and lasting change.

One priesthood leader in the Book of Mormon saw people sorrowing and thought is was evidence of their readiness for changing their ways. He later teaches that heavy sorrow is not the only prerequisite for repentance. Mormon wrote, "Behold this my joy was vain, for their sorrowing was not unto repentance, because of the goodness of God; but it was rather the sorrowing of the damned, because the Lord would not always suffer them to take happiness in sin" (Mormon 2:13).

Time to build the infrastructure of gratitude for the Savior and His healing grace comes when appreciation renders a kind and service-oriented heart. It comes over time when feelings of gratitude cleanse and heal our hearts and minds. It requires time to bring sustained peace, warmth, and love to the sinner's innermost parts. Although beginning down the road after committing serious infractions against Heavenly Father's commandments brings relief and hope for a new start, it is necessary to continue further by building a stronger foundation of gratitude. As stated by Elder Hales, "Gratitude is also the foundation upon which repentance is built. The Atonement brought mercy through repentance to balance justice" (Robert D. Hales, "Gratitude for the Goodness of God," *Ensign*, May 1992).

The foundation of gratitude helps us be ready to be forgiven and to experience the lasting change we seek. Elder Hales also taught,

> Gratitude expressed to our Heavenly Father in prayer for what we have brings a calming peace—a peace which allows us to not canker our souls for what we don't have. Gratitude brings a peace that helps us overcome the pain of adversity and failure. Gratitude on a daily basis means we express appreciation for what we have now without qualification for what we had in the past or desire in the future. A recognition of and appreciation for our gifts and talents which have been given also allows us to acknowledge the need for help and assistance from the gifts and talents possessed by others. (Ibid.)

It is important to remember that priesthood leaders are given the insight and revelation to help us navigate the road to repentance. Timing is up to the Lord and His inspired and authorized servants who act under the direction of the Apostles from priesthood handbooks and from the voice of conference. Our priesthood leaders will be inspired to provide the specific guidance in the repentance process for serious sin. The influence and presence of the Holy Ghost in our lives will confirm forgiveness in our repentance of less serious matters.

The message of this chapter is to establish the truth that appreciation and heartfelt gratitude for the opportunity we have to repent and be forgiven of all sins is foundational. Just as the foundation for a tool shed takes less time to create than the complicated dynamics associated with the building of the gigantic BYU–Idaho Center, so it is with sin and repentance. In all cases, love for the Savior, appreciation for His atoning sacrifice, and gratitude to Heavenly Father provide the basis for lasting repentance.

## Self-Examination for Greater Gratitude

1. Take a few minutes the next time you write in your journal to express your gratitude for the Savior, for His Atonement, and for your Heavenly Father, who loves you.
2. Have you felt profound appreciation and the subsequent peace from repentance and forgiveness in your life? Who needs to hear your testimony of that truth?
3. How can you take steps toward daily repentance by having a more thankful heart?

## Scriptures for Consideration and Marking

Mormon 2:13
Acts 27:35
2 Corinthians 4:15
Matthew 15:36
Mosiah 24:13–16

## Parting Thought

I have a testimony based on experience that has taught me that when my heart is full of gratitude for God, the Savior, and my fellowman, I am inclined to be more complete and frequent in my desire to repent. A great priesthood leader in my life once taught me that the definition of a righteous person is someone who is in a constant state of repentance. If that is true, then living with a thankful heart positions us to become more righteous, because we feel more disposed to seek peace and cleanliness through repentance. May we seek to develop and maintain a thankful heart.

# 15

# Submission and Peace

---

"The kind of gratitude that receives even tribulations with thanksgiving requires a broken heart and a contrite spirit, humility to accept that which we cannot change, willingness to turn everything over to the Lord—even when we do not understand, thankfulness for hidden opportunities yet to be revealed. Then comes a sense of peace." (Bonnie D. Parkin, "Gratitude: A Path to Happiness," *Ensign*, May 2007)

---

One of the blessings I'm most thankful for is to have married into a family where I am treated like a son and a brother instead of an in-law. As family, we feel safe and are able to share candid and real feelings of our hearts. Over the years, Dale, my brother-in-law, and I have shared many personal feelings and observations about life and the pursuit of our dreams. A few years ago in the prime of his professional life, he was diagnosed with stage-four colon cancer. Priesthood blessings, faith, and time produced a miracle, and it appears he is on the road to becoming completely cancer free. Their finances are sufficient and their hearts prepared to serve a full-time mission. Dale shared with me the essence of a journal entry. Permission was given to share it in this chapter. It is useful in accenting the teachings of Sister Parkin in the quote above.

> Ten days after our papers had been submitted, our stake president gently notified us that because of a previous health concern, missionary medical would not consider us for a foreign assignment. We were heartbroken and devastated. I felt confident in my recovered health through sweet yet powerful spiritual experiences. Further, it had felt as though the

Lord was guiding us toward the experience in Africa. We did all we could to communicate that, but finally I felt we must now turn our hearts toward aligning with the will of the Lord. . . .

We applied ourselves diligently to our focus of offering ourselves up to the Lord and expressing our pleas that He help us totally yield our hearts to Him. We felt the Lord had heard our prayer that we desired to go to Africa, but we felt it was unnecessary to repeat that plea. During three different temple sessions, I felt that the Lord knows me and loves me and that I could accept His divine will in our forthcoming call. This was moving and very strengthening. . . .

Through the following days, I felt good about my thoughts and willingness to yield my heart to God. I was succeeding. But a week later, I began to struggle again. My mind became focused on the decision and input of missionary medical and how they did not acknowledge my miracle in health. I found myself being stirred up again in my heart. I sought to put it out of my mind, but without much success. A visit to the temple and pleadings to the Lord strengthened me again.

On January 8, 2015, Julie retrieved the call from our mailbox, and we spent a *long* afternoon awaiting the arrival of our children. I continued to pray privately that I would align with His will, but deep in my mind I expected that the Lord would accept our offering, much as He had done with my cancer journey, and honor us by sending us to Africa. I sought to put those thoughts out of my mind, and I was excited for the blessed journey ahead. With the family gathered, Julie read the call: "You are hereby called to labor in the Texas Fort Worth Mission. Your primary assignment is to labor in the Denton Texas CES Program as a CES Specialist."

I was deeply heartbroken but sought, with great effort, to put a smile on my face. Julie was excited and carried me in demonstrating enthusiasm. The night was not restful. My dreams of Africa were dashed. The miracle I expected had not materialized. I knew, however, that I had pledged and would accept the Lord's will. I was under covenant to do so. This I would do! . . .

I awoke still aching and without enthusiasm. I did not feel excited to tell the people on our "let us know" list. . . . While I struggled, Julie had a steady feeling of excitement and enthusiasm. As I have many times, I marveled at my bride's strength and spiritual leadership in our relationship!

That night I did not welcome thoughts of another restless night. At this point, my emotional stress was less about the call and more about my weakness and how disappointed the Lord must be in me. I felt I had acted very childish and knew my behavior was not pleasing to Him. Why after sixty-three years had I not grown up?

While I seemed to have awakened numerous times, the night was not restless. In fact, it was quite the opposite. Each time I awoke, my mind and heart felt an excitement about our mission call to Denton. When I arose in the morning, I felt excited, enriched, and healed of that which had troubled me since the call. The Lord helped me understand through the night that He had a special need for Julie and me in Denton in the CES program. This was His call and was not about my health. These manifestations of the Spirit were a tremendous spiritual gift and blessing to me that I shall never forget.

I have burned with excitement about our call every day since this experience. It is so comforting to know that the Lord needs us in Texas for a sacred purpose, and not because I am somehow too broken to serve in Africa. The divine process in our call has been rich in spiritual refinement as I was tutored by a patient and nurturing Father in Heaven. I feel so grateful that I learned a rich lesson in yielding myself to the will of God. Our thankful hearts anticipate learning even more of why we were called to serve Him and His children in Denton, Texas. (Dale R. Bond, personal journal entry, used with permission)

## Self-Examination for Greater Gratitude

1. What experiences have you had that have caused you to submit your will to Father in Heaven and later receive peace? Have you recorded it in your journal and shared it with family and friends?
2. Who do you know who might be going through lessons in their own lives who might be blessed by understanding the principles and concepts in this chapter? How can you share?
3. Is there a present issue in your life that requires submission and gratitude for some life-shaping challenge (great or small)?

## Scriptures for Consideration and Marking

Proverbs 3:5
D&C 6:36
3 Nephi 10:10
John 14:27
D&C 6:20

## Parting Thought

I have learned that Heavenly Father and His Son, Jesus Christ, aided by the Holy Ghost, have but one mission and purpose. They are united in giving us experiences and helping us learn eternally important lessons in the school and laboratory of earth life. Ultimately Their purpose and glory is to bring to pass that we will live forever (have immortality) and become like Them and have a god life (merit eternal life). All of our experiences are calculated to that end. May we learn our lessons well and become as He is.

# 16

# The Blessings of the Restoration

"We can best express our gratitude for this glorious fulness [of the restored gospel] by developing a more full love for all of humankind. And why not, for the Restoration tells us who our neighbors really are! Let our gratitude likewise be expressed by striving to become, attribute by attribute, more and more as Jesus is." (Neal A. Maxwell, "'From the Beginning,'" *Ensign*, November 1993, 20)

Several years ago I was asked to develop a one-semester religion class for nonmembers attending Ricks College. The course was to be called Religion 100: Introduction to Mormonism. It was designed to introduce students with little or no background in the Church to the basic teachings of the restored gospel. The teaching was not to proselyte in any way but to provide a course in which nonmembers or new members of the Church could come to understand what their member friends believe, why so many choose to serve missions, and what temple marriage is, and to help them to learn the history and background of the Church.

Most of the students in the class were from foreign countries, friends of LDS students in high school, or athletes playing their sport at Ricks College. One morning after class, a student athlete approached me and asked if he could visit for a few minutes in my office. After sitting down, he said, "I don't know what's happening to me. I'm feeling some very positive feelings about the Mormon Church. My family warned me about this when I came. They said you all would attack me and try to make me a Mormon. Well, that hasn't happened. No one is trying to convince me of anything. But I'm feeling something, and I don't really want to feel it." After a response and general discussion, he leaned over to get a little closer to me and asked, "Brother, if you were to find out today that Joseph Smith was a hoax, the Book of Mormon therefore is not true, and that the Mormon Church is just like all the other churches—would you still be a Mormon?" I responded, "So what you are asking is that if the Mormon Church is not the only true church on earth and is just another nice church like the Baptist, Catholic, Methodist, or the other nine hundred plus Christian churches, would I still be a Mormon? Is that correct?" He affirmed, "Yes, that's what I'm asking." I paused for a few moments and then said to him, "That's a difficult question!" He seemed pleased. "It's difficult because I feel so strongly that Joseph is a prophet and that the Book of Mormon is true that I can't easily respond, but yes, I would still be a Mormon." He inquisitively responded with, "You would?"

I then listed several reasons why I would be a Mormon. When I moved my family from Gilbert, Arizona, to Farmington Hills, Michigan, and then again from Michigan to Rexburg, in one single telephone call, our ninth grade daughter had a half dozen girl friends and a dozen boy peers we could trust to watch out for her. With that same phone call, my seventh grade son had a Scout troop and a deacons quorum of a dozen boys or more. All eight of my children immediately had two or three adult men or women who would assist my wife and I in caring for their progress. My wife immediately had friends and a society of good women with whom to associate.

My student was playing for Ricks on a basketball scholarship, so I added, "And with one more telephone call, I would have a place to play and group of guys who would welcome me to play hoop the following morning." He chuckled and said, "Well, then it must be true."

I want to live a long and healthy life. This is a religion that embraces a careful health code. It's never been a big temptation for me to smoke, drink, or fool around with drugs. I want that same standard for my children.

The welfare program teaches us to help those in need and gives us a variety of ways to do that through monthly donations and actual service. There is a program that points us toward our roots—where our family comes from—and it helps us bind generations. There are programs for children, youth, and adults to improve their lives and to become educated.

While my education has helped me to make a living, my mission has changed my life in every good way. I learned more about life serving a two-year mission in Mexico than I ever learned in getting my university degrees.

My friendship, courtship, temple marriage, and life with my sweetheart have been the greatest blessings of my life, which would not be without the blessings of the Church and its organization. In our case, we began our friendship when we were ten years old in the Church program for children.

I then summarized, "I've given you a dozen social reasons why I would be a Mormon. But none are the real reason. The reason your question is difficult to answer is only because I can't take away what I already know. It's like if you were to ask me if I believed in sunlight and wind. I have seen the sun, felt it's warmth, and experienced the bitter winds of Rexburg." He moaned and said, "Yeah, me too!" I continued, "So if you were to ask me to pretend I'd never seen the sun or felt the cold winds of Idaho, I would have to say I can't pretend I haven't seen or felt those two intangibles because I have. Does that make sense?" He replied affirmatively.

Then I followed, "My friend, The Church of Jesus Christ of Latter-day Saints is the restored Church of Jesus Christ. God lives and loves us—you and me. His doctrine is centered in His plan. As you remember from class we call it the plan of salvation, or sometimes we just call it the great plan of happiness. That plan has given me framework to help me deal with the death of a brother and two nephews and the daily demands of a special needs daughter. The plan and the gospel help me to know who you are and why I love you and want the best for you and your future spouse. It helps me to understand why you are an important link to the past generations in your family and also those who will yet come."

I continued, "Joseph Smith was a prophet. He didn't start this Church; he restored it. As a part of the Restoration, he received metal plates inscribed with writing and translated them by the power and will of Heavenly Father. The Book of Mormon is exactly what he said it is, and it's true. The heavens are not closed. We have a living prophet with twelve Apostles. We have priesthood authority, which brings me, my family, and all believers and possessors great blessings."

I concluded by saying, "I love this Church and its restored gospel, and I want others to have it too. That may be why your parents were concerned by your coming here. Because all of us who know what it is love it, and we want everyone to know about it. Does that answer your question?" I said with a smile. What a sweet feeling to acknowledge and count our blessings from the restored gospel of Jesus Christ.

**Self-Examination for Greater Gratitude**

1. What are your feelings about the restored gospel? Have you shared those feelings with family and loved ones recently?
2. How can you show others how you feel about how you feel about them and the blessings of the gospel?
3. When will you express your love for God, His gospel, His Son, and those you care for?

## Scriptures for Consideration and Marking

Daniel 2:44–45
Revelations 14:6
Alma 26:11–13, 16
Acts 3:21
Alma 36:17–21
Alma 9:20–22

## Parting Thought

I had a little project a few years ago to look at the final testimonies of special witnesses. I appreciate so much one of the last public witnesses given by ninety-seven-year-old David B. Haight. He said,

> I wish at this time to pay tribute and express gratitude to my Heavenly Father for the blessings I've received all the years of my life—for having been born of goodly parents and raised in a goodly home. . . . And so I'm grateful to my Heavenly Father for the blessings that I have had. I bear witness of Him, that I know that He is our Father and that Jesus is the Christ, the Son of the living God, the Creator, and the Savior of all of mankind. I am grateful for that majestic role He has played in the Creation and the establishing of the gospel on the earth and for the opportunity that brings to mankind, if they will listen, to hear and to understand and to have the blessings of heaven if they merit them and to live in such a way that the gospel becomes a great part of their life. (David B. Haight, "Were There Not Ten Cleansed?" *Ensign*, November 2002)

I want my own family, you, and others to know how thankful I am for the restored gospel of Jesus Christ.

# 17

# Thankfulness and Gratitude

"Gratitude is the feeling itself. That is in the heart. Thankfulness is measured by the number of words; gratitude is measured by the nature of our actions. Thankfulness is the beginning of gratitude; gratitude the completion of thankfulness." (David O. McKay, "An Expression of Gratitude," in *Conference Report*, October 1955, 4–9)

One of the sweet memories I have while serving as a bishop was the kind, sweet, loving heart of a young man in his mid-twenties named Ricky. He and his aging mother faithfully attended church each week like most others, but Ricky came to worship with something that was infectious and lifting—love and kindness toward everyone. Living with Down syndrome was undoubtedly a challenge for both Ricky and his mother. But our lives were all enriched by his sweet, innocent simplicity. Ricky just loved the people in our ward no matter their age, race, or gender. I can't remember if he was formally called to be the greeter, but in his own official capacity he took his place at the door to shake hands and be the first one to say hello to all those who set foot in the chapel. Since there were two doors entering the chapel, he would alternate weekly from one side to the other so as not to miss anyone during the month.

He was short of stature and rather portly. His speech was not clear enough to understand, but the love in his enlarging heart, combined with his warm chubby hands, was enough to brighten our day and get us ready for taking the sacrament and remembering the attributes of Jesus Christ. It was a given that the seats on the bench nearest the door were reserved for Ricky and his mother.

Postured there, when someone needed to leave the meeting with a crying child, he was there to serve by opening and closing the door.

On the first Sunday of each month he arrived at church a little earlier than usual. It was fast Sunday and he came not only to care for his ushering duties but also to share his love through his testimony. When the bishopric turned the meeting to the members for the bearing of testimonies, everyone knew that Ricky was first. The millisecond he heard "We will now turn the time to you for the bearing of testimonies," he would stand and walk boldly down the aisle to take his place at the pulpit, where he would try to communicate his heartfelt love to the members of the ward family.

In the few minutes he shared, it was difficult to understand anything he said. The words were garbled at best, except for one short phrase that always exited his mouth and heart clearly. I loved listening and anticipating through the seeming sentences of jumbled sounds for the one phrase we could all hear, understand, and feel: "I love da peoples." He would start again in the language none in the congregation could understand until we heard again "I love da peoples." And again, and again. In the last fifteen seconds of his testimony, he always became emotional and, through tears and sobbing, leaned over the pulpit and said, "I love da peoples," followed by a few more garbled words concluding with "Jesus Christ, Amen." His testimony and message weren't complete until he turned to me, the bishop, sitting sat tall in my chair so Ricky's short stature had to lean over only slightly to put his wet, teary face on my cheek. Still sobbing, he whispered in my ear one single word, *love*. He then nobly and stoically walked back to his place on the bench next to his mother to resume his duty at the door.

Currently my life is blessed in me remembering Ricky from over thirty years ago because of one of his younger kindred spirits. Jared is another Saint with Down syndrome. He is now a priesthood holder in his late twenties and a giver of love. He is stationed every Saturday morning at the west door of the Rexburg Temple. As patrons enter, he opens the door and is first to welcome them. Like Ricky, he seems to say with every act of simple temple service, "I love da peoples."

For over four decades I have not heard a perceptible word from Chantel, our daughter diagnosed with Rett syndrome. Sometimes she makes sounds, but she never speaks a word. However, when she looks at me as I either provide some small act of service for her or just open my arms up wide to invite her to receive my hug, there's something in her eyes that communicates from her heart, "I love da people, and you, and Mom, and everybody." What a blessing Chantel is to our home and family.

As stated in the opening quote, "Gratitude is the feeling itself. That is in the heart. Thankfulness is measured by the number of words; gratitude is measured by the nature of our actions. Thankfulness is the beginning of gratitude; gratitude the completion of thankfulness." President David O. McKay also added, "Gratitude is the heart's recognition of kindness that the lips cannot repay." (Ibid.)

It is apparent that in the examples of Ricky, Jared, and Chantel that gratitude is the feeling of kindness. Their simple words, if any, are the uncomplicated expressions of what's in their hearts. "I love da peoples" are words. Their actions and eyes are the manifestation of what they feel.

I am grateful for the Rickys, Jareds, and Chantels of the world who are ideal, consummate, and visual models for us to pattern our lives after. They exemplify the prophetic teaching of President McKay. May we have gratitude and thankful hearts as we show love for "da peoples."

## Self-Examination for Greater Gratitude

1. How would you rate your expression of gratitude through your actions?
2. How do rate your expression of thankfulness through your words to others?
3. What can you do today, this week, and this month to feel and show more gratitude and express more from your thankful heart?

## Scriptures for Consideration and Marking

D&C 78:19
Psalm 105:1–2
Daniel 6:10
Luke 12:48
Psalm 136:2

## Parting Thought

I love the words of Elder Jeffrey R. Holland when he expressed gratitude to the members of the Church as well as to those not of our faith:

> My thanks to all you wonderful members of the Church—and legions of good people not of our faith—for proving every day of your life that the pure love of Christ "never faileth." No one of you is insignificant, in part because you make the gospel of Jesus Christ what it is—a living reminder of His grace and mercy, a private but powerful manifestation in small villages and large cities of the good He did and the life He gave bringing peace and salvation to other people. . . . Brothers and sisters, seeing your example, I pledge anew my determination to be better, to be more faithful—more kind and devoted, more charitable and true as our Father in Heaven is and as so many of you already are. This I pray in the name of our Great Exemplar in all things—even the

name of the Lord Jesus Christ—amen. (Jeffrey R. Holland, "Because of Your Faith," *Ensign*, November 2010)

# 18
# His Divine Companionship

"My prayer was, 'Give me a miracle,' you know? 'Solve this problem.' And it took a while to finally come to the point of saying, 'I'm content to get a daily help and let it take what time it takes, knowing that I can rely upon God.' And it's been a blessing to me ever since to have had that rather harrowing experience because of what it meant for my relationship with Him. Maybe the greater blessing for us is to have to walk through it with Him." (D. Todd Christofferson, "Daily Bread: Experience," *Mormon Messages*, episode 105)

The Lord has blessed my life by letting me know and associate with many great people. I hope you feel the same way. One of those extraordinary people was Jeffrey Jensen of Murray, Utah. Because of visa problems, I did not travel to my field of labor with a group of missionaries as most do. My group left while I awaited in Provo for my visa. Several weeks later, I arrived alone in one of the largest cities of the world without a companion, speaking little Spanish. After going through the rigors of the governmental customs and checkpoints at the airport, in a language I didn't understand, I finally made it through to see three office missionaries waiting for me. They explained that normally we would go to the mission home and have some orientation with the mission president, but this time would be different. My mission president, Gordon Romney, was in the far north of the mission conducting interviews. So after a brief stop at the mission home, they took me right to my area. After a hair-raising ride through the bustling traffic dominated primarily by taxis, I was delivered to my new home and companion in the part of the city known as Industrial. I have since prayed that my own missionary children could have a first companion like Elder Jensen.

"Let's set your bags by your bed; you can unpack when we get back tonight," he said. We went straight to work despite my travel fatigue and culture shock. When we arrived at the designated area where he and his former companion had been methodically tracting for the previous weeks, Elder Jensen said, "Okay, I'll take the first door, and then I want you to take the next nine or ten." I agreed but felt there was some inequity involved. He explained, "We need to do all we can to help the Lord help you to become an effective missionary." Elder Jensen took the first door. In his perfect two-year-plus Spanish, he rattled off a short dialog and began asking questions and engaging in conversation. I was soon lost, not understanding my companion or those at the door. When it came my turn, I gave my short memorized door approach learned at the LTM (language training mission). I asked the scripted question, and the person answered speaking a hundred words a minute. I didn't understand anything! I looked at my trainer for help, and he just whispered, "You're doing fine. Ask it a different way." Each door was the same. When I looked to him for help, he said, "You're doing fine, Elder. You're doing fine." That was honestly frustrating for me, and I didn't always appreciate his training methods. But I could feel myself getting better. For me, Spanish was difficult to learn. Even as I got better, there would be times in those early months when all of a sudden the curtains would drop on my Spanish-speaking mind and I couldn't remember how to speak, let alone process what the person was saying to me. It's like my brain just said, "I'm done. I can't do it anymore. I need a rest."

One particular late afternoon three months later, we were teaching the Guevarras, a wonderful family who were prepared and progressing well. Though I had improved substantially since those first days, I had one of those moments when the curtains dropped and my capacity to speak or understand went on hold. We were teaching a fourth or fifth lesson, and it was an important time in the Guevarras progress. When my mind stopped working, I discreetly turned to Elder Jensen and said, "I'm lost. Can you take over?" Elder Jensen looked straight ahead at this wonderful family and whispered out of the side of his mouth, "You're doing fine, Elder. You're doing just fine." Well, I wasn't doing just fine. I knew it, and so did he. A precious family was a stake here. I managed to remain controlled through the rest of that discussion, but I was embarrassed and not happy with Elder Jensen.

When we left the home later and began our walk to the next appointment, I felt it was time to tell my companion off. "Elder, don't ever do that again. I was lost and needed your help. I couldn't speak, and I couldn't understand. When I ask you for help, give it to me!" Elder Jensen waited until I was done lecturing and then replied, "Elder Christensen, you are becoming a good missionary, but you need to remember that you aren't the teacher anyway. The Spirit is the real teacher. The Guevarras were feeling it, despite your struggling. Yes, they were feeling it, and you were doing just fine."

That's the way it was for the next four months. I have no doubt that when I opened my mouth on those first doors, armed only with my LTM Spanish, Elder Jensen knew he was in for a challenge. But Elder Jensen knew that rescuing me every time I stumbled or that taking over each time I felt a little linguistic fatigue would not help me grow and become what he envisioned I could become. Further and most important, he waited until the time was right (and I was ready) to teach me who the real teacher was. I don't know if I ever really became the missionary and teacher Elder Jensen saw in me. But I do know I loved being a missionary and a president over 563 missionaries in Chile and well over 2,000 missionaries in the Guatemala MTC.

I believe part of that love came from having Elder Jensen figuratively take me by the hand and walk with me through the process of becoming a missionary and a teacher. We become better acquainted with the Lord when He walks with us and supports us while we take on our challenges and meet up with our adversities. He refrains from rescuing us in times when we would prefer reprieve or a miracle to take our discomfort away. In His wisdom, He knows our greatest growth and understanding will come in the peak of the storm.

I will be forever thankful for Elder Jensen and for a Father in Heaven who knows that "the greater blessing for us is to have to walk through it with Him" (D. Todd Christofferson, "Daily Bread: Experience," *Mormon Messages*, episode 105).

## Self-Examination for Greater Gratitude

1. Are you able to see when the Lord was with you during a moment or season of adversity, but He let you grow instead of removing the challenge from you? When?
2. Consider sharing your experiences of the question above in your journal. Someone in the future will be blessed by your testimony.
3. Whom do you know right now who feels abandoned and is begging for a miracle? Share Elder Christofferson's quote with that person.

## Scriptures for Consideration and Marking

D&C 121–122
Job 1:22
D&C 46:32
Genesis 22:1–18
Colossians 3:17

## Parting Thought

There many stories of the Mormon handcart pioneers who related how in the moments of their greatest adversities they felt help from those on the other side of the veil walking with them through their challenges—not taking the entire load. President Uchtdorf once said, "We can learn this from the fearless handcart pioneers who, by their own strength, pulled their meager belongings in handcarts across the scorching plains and through the snows of the high mountain passes to escape persecution, and then expressed their gratitude in peaceful worship in the Salt Lake Valley" (Dieter F. Uchtdorf, "Reconciliation and Thanksgiving," talk at the Salt Lake Rotary Club, November 19, 2013).

# 19

# *Prayers of Gratitude*

"The most meaningful and spiritual prayers I have experienced contained many expressions of thanks and few, if any, requests." (David A. Bednar, "Pray Always," *Ensign*, November 2008)

How do we learn to live daily with a thankful heart? How do we remain thankful through the thick and thin of life? How do we recognize our multitude of blessings and express gratitude at least as much as we ask or request more blessings? Why is there a significant imbalance between thankers and requesters?

We should never discount or diminish the fact that Heavenly Father has encouraged us to ask and seek for resolutions to our problems and yearnings of the heart. However, the balance between having gratitude for our blessings and requesting more falls in favor of the nearly constant appeal for more. One of Elder Neal A. Maxwell's teachings used earlier in this book seems appropriate here as well: "Mortal mathematics . . . is forever mistaking who and what counts. Even so, we should be more quick to express genuine appreciation. . . . The arithmetic of appreciation is far less practiced and known than the multiplication tables" (*The Neal A Maxwell Quote Book*, edited by Cory H. Maxwell [Salt Lake City: Bookcraft, 1997], 147). While we should comply with Father's requests to ask Him, it's also true we should avoid developing "gimmee syndrome." Excessive "Give me this" or "Give us more of that" easily develops into the "gimmee syndrome."

The antithesis of being incessant and relentless beggars is simply having a thankful heart, which sees the Lord's hand in all things. One of the greatest of examples of a thankful heart is my sister Janice.

She's been such a special angel that I've mentioned her in other writings, talks, and lessons over the years. Her example is profoundly seated in the attitude of gratitude. In her early teen years, Janice contracted polio, which left her with only partial use of her arms and one of her legs. A leg brace and crutch were necessary for her to function in her limited movement. My sister Carole, just a year older than Janice, also came down with polio. Jan was the first to be rushed to the hospital and placed in an iron lung to help her survive limited breathing capacity. A few days later, Carole joined her and they were confined to a polio ward. In that setting, Jan expressed gratitude: "Heavenly Father is so good to us to allow us to be together so that we can help and encourage one another." She saw the Lord's hand in her circumstance and with a thankful heart acknowledged it.

Most people expected Jan to never marry and certainly to never have children. But, she did marry and raised seven children while fulfilling time- and energy-consuming Church callings, like Relief Society president and stake missionary. She was blessed with six boys, one daughter, and a husband who was equally yoked serving in the Lord's kingdom.

One summer day, Jan's husband, Marv, drove to the Grand Canyon to pick up boys from the ward who had completed a weeklong hike. He decided to take two of his youngest boys along for the ride. They and two other cars met the boys and their weary leaders at the appointed trailhead. Everyone loaded up and started on the journey home. Traveling southbound on the freeway near Cottonwood, Arizona, they met an intoxicated driver going nearly ninety miles per hour northbound in the southbound lanes. The first two vehicles navigated out of the way of the oncoming time bomb, but Marv's vehicle, occupied by eight passengers, met it in a head-on crash. One adult advisor and three youth died, including Jan's two sons. The moment she learned about the accident and that her boys were dead, she said, "I'm so thankful that our two boys could go and be together in the next chapter of their progression beyond the veil. They are just less than a year apart in age."

Marv was in critical condition, holding on to life at every breath. He was in a coma and not aware of the boys' deaths or their funeral. After the funeral, Jan began a vigil at Marv's bedside. One of the nurses fixed her a special chair with pillows to make her more comfortable. She leaned against the armrest to reposition herself and suddenly realized there was no armrest. She lost her balance and fell to the floor, breaking her thighbone. After surgery, pin insertion, and bone repair, they put her in the room with Marv. She now lay in the hospital bed next to her husband's. She said, "The Lord is so good to me. He allowed me to come here and be next to my husband so that we can help get him better." In Janice's presence, Marv rallied and miraculously recovered.

Janice lived with a thankful heart. Developing a thankful heart and attitude of gratitude helps us to focus more upon the blessings given us and less upon the things we don't have. We are less likely to become excessive in wanting for more when we are grateful for what God has already given us.

Elder Maxwell once taught, "Small minds forget large blessing? Proud minds ceaselessly inquire of God. . . . 'What have you done for me lately?' If one is without the faith that remembers, past benefactions are forgotten because of present deprivations. For the meek and faithful, miracles . . . including blessings large and small . . . add to their gratitude and wonder. As we pray in an attitude of complete discipleship, we are swallowed up in gratitude for what he has already given" (Neal A. Maxwell, *Men and Women of Christ* [Salt Lake City: Bookcraft, 1991]).

Perhaps the best place to begin and maintain this attribute is in our prayer life. Elder Bednar suggests, "Let me recommend that periodically you and I offer a prayer in which we only give thanks and express gratitude. Ask for nothing; simply let our souls rejoice and strive to communicate appreciation with all the energy of our hearts" (David A. Bednar, "Pray Always," *Ensign*, November 2008). His invitation to do this periodically has no timetable. I have found that anytime I start to notice the balance of requests seem to rival my awareness of blessings, it's time for a gratitude prayer.

## Self-Examination for Greater Gratitude

1. If you are not already aware, do a little listening to yourself in your prayers. Make sure you are grateful in your expressions of appreciation to the Lord for your many blessings.
2. Make a list of your blessings. Forget what you need or want right now. Drill down deep into the well of gratitude and make visible written words and phrases of all your blessings. Keep expanding the list as you remember blessings. Maintain it and add to it with a watchful, spiritual eye.
3. Besides our Heavenly Father, the Giver of all blessings, whom of His children do you need to thank for what they've done for you? Write a note, make a call, or send a text today to someone who helped Heavenly Father answer your prayers.

## Scriptures for Consideration and Marking

Luke 17:11–19
Psalm 30:12
Alma 26:37
2 Corinthians 9:15
1 Thessalonians 5:18

## Parting Thought

Developing a thankful heart is a process. The natural man, who is an enemy to God (Mosiah 3:19), has the tendency to be narcissistic. With the natural man, we can become like Korihor in the Book of Mormon and buy into the notion that by the brilliant management of the creature, we achieve, attain, and succeed. It is easy to become egocentric in what we do and how we do it. I once heard someone say that *ego* is really an acronym for "edging God out." The person who has a thankful heart is one who puts off the natural man by acknowledging God in all things and remembering that He is the fountain of all blessings.

# 20
# Abundance

"I invite you . . . to think abundantly. I love the word *abundant*; it has lots of soft sound and seems to go along with . . . the harvest and gathering in. Thinking abundantly means knowing that there is more than enough for everyone. Abundant thinking is full of gratitude for what you have and delight in what others have." (Virginia Pearce, "Of Sound Mind," Brigham Young University–Hawaii devotional, October 23, 2012)

I love to study the meaning of words. *Abundance* means plenteousness, overflowing, and a quantity more than sufficient. The antithesis of *abundance* is *scarcity*. Unlike the word *abundance*, *scarcity* screams shortage, deficiency, and want.

Through the lens of abundance, we see there is no end to the blessings available to His children. Conversely through the lens of scarcity, we feel that if one person gets a blessing, that's one less available. Scarcity also breeds another unhealthy viewpoint that I call the "If I had, then I could" syndrome. It spawns phrases in our psyche like "If I just had more money, then I'd be happy" or "If I had a new car, then I'd appear more successful" or "If my kids would not do that, then we could be a happy family." Scarcity mentality and the "If I had, then I could" syndrome are thieves of happiness. Thinking abundantly reminds us to look at all heaven has given us and with a thankful heart to know that Heavenly Father gives an endless multitude of tender mercies. The only thing it requires is to change our seat and renew our perspective.

I recall on more than one occasion observing our children during the great season of being three to six years old. One such time, we were all watching Aaron open birthday gifts. With the opening of each gift, comments filled the room, especially from one little sister, Chenae, who would say with heartfelt joy, "Oh Aaron, that's so cool." You could see in her eyes a genuine pleasure and gladness for Aaron's good fortune. It was a pleasure to see the delight she portrayed. Something happens when we grow older. The joy described above is somehow replaced with "How come she got that and I only got this?" or "It's not fair!" Happiness for others can be replaced with envy, coveting, and the "If I had, then I could" syndrome.

Debbie and Deena lived across the street from one another. Both were young mothers whose husbands were in the "business building" phase of their professional lives. Both husbands were also in demanding roles in their Church callings and a bit overwhelmed with fatherhood. Likewise, Debbie and Deena were in the phase of motherhood where all the children were young and still at home, and they were engaged in callings, PTA, and community activity. They had an early morning walking routine where they would get out and walk a couple of miles before sunrise to take care of their health and also talk about life and enjoy mutual therapy.

One morning as they walked and talked, Deena slid into a monologue recounting her current life challenges in a spirit of murmuring. "I'm really fatigued from not having enough money to pay bills. We have to be really careful about what we spend on groceries, and dealing with the constant demands of the kids is overwhelming to say the least. My Church calling is wiping me out, and my husband is so busy right now." They turned the corner and walked up another long street. When Deena paused, Debbie politely and sweetly said, "May I tell you what I see from across the street?" Deena responded, "Sure." Debbie went on to list all the good things she saw about Deena and her family from a distance: wonderful children; folks who have sufficient for their needs; people doing well in their Church assignments; a wonderful, loving couple who support each other. The list went on. As they finished their two miles, Deena was lifted, grateful for the perspective, and reminded of her blessings.

Sometimes when we are in the trenches of life, slaving away, working at making a living, raising families, or whatever demands consume our attention, we can slip into the mode of feeling deprived. We become covertly obsessed with our own inadequacies and shortcomings. When we are in the scarcity mentality mode, we can only be happy if we get something someone else doesn't have. Or we find ways to mentally sabotage the success of others, at least in our own minds. If not checked, we can easily miss the more accurate view others see from across the street.

I agree with Sister Pearce in the opening quote when she said, "I love the word *abundant*. . . . Thinking abundantly means knowing that there is more than enough for everyone. Abundant thinking is full of gratitude for what you have and delight in what others have." Heavenly Father wants to give us blessings, assurances of His love, and help along our way. After all, His whole purpose and glory is to give us all that He has. If He gives us all that He has, then we could interpret that He won't have anything left for Himself. Not so, not even close. His blessing and abundance is plenty and enough for all.

### Self-Examination for Greater Gratitude

1. Are you blessed with abundance mentality or plagued with scarcity attitudes?
2. How can you improve your ability to see the blessings and abundance Heavenly Father has and will give?
3. How can you teach those closest to you about that abundance?

## Scriptures for Consideration and Marking

Alma 9:19
John 10:10
D&C 104:16–18

## Parting Thought

The Lord said,

> But it must needs be done in mine own way; and behold this is the way that I, the Lord, have decreed to provide for my saints, that the poor shall be exalted, in that the rich are made low.
>
> For the earth is full, and there is enough and to spare; yea, I prepared all things, and have given unto the children of men to be agents unto themselves.
>
> Therefore, if any man shall take of the abundance which I have made, and impart not his portion, according to the law of my gospel, unto the poor and the needy, he shall, with the wicked, lift up his eyes in hell, being in torment. (D&C 104:16–18)

Heavenly Father is the Master of abundant living. May we be grateful for His promises of abundance and show our thankful hearts by sharing it with others and having joy in the success and happiness of His children.

## 21

# The Test of Our Devotion and Gratitude

"In our hearts do we feel a sense of gratitude and devotion to the Father? Are we of one heart with Him to whom we owe everything? The test of our devotion to the Lord seems to be the way we serve Him." (L. Tom Perry, "Youth of the Noble Birthright," *Ensign*, November 1998)

One of the most extraordinary missionaries in our experience in Chile was a young man who entered the mission with an obedient heart, a great work ethic, and the perfect combination of confidence and charisma. From the moment I saw him, I expected a high level of service and success for him as a missionary.

A few weeks later in our regular interview, he said, "All I've ever wanted is to be a great missionary! I've looked forward to this day for as long as I can remember. But I'm not having a very good experience." I suspected culture shock, because I knew it could not be his companion, who was one of the best. "President, I don't love these people. In fact, I don't even like them. Their dogs are mangy and dirty. In fact they might as well be dogs to me! I don't hate the people, but I sure don't feel love for them. What should I do?" he pleaded.

We visited for a while, and I encouraged him to fast, pray, and look for every opportunity to serve the people, not just teach them. Roughly six weeks passed with me contacting him four or five times in between. Each time he'd report that he was doing a little better.

Our next interview was preceded by rumors from other missionaries that this wonderful elder was not only doing better but was also talking to everyone and offering to serve people at every opportunity. He entered the room with a controlled smile and a bounce in his step. "President, I'm cured! I love these people! I'm having a great experience finally. I still don't like their dogs, but the people are awesome. I'm so happy."

What happened? Why the change in just six weeks? First, he was seeking and had a desire in his heart to change. I believe he turned the corner when he added the gift of service to his obedience, diligence, good looks, and people skills.

President Spencer W. Kimball taught,

> Service to others deepens and sweetens this life while we are preparing to live in a better world. It is by serving that we learn to serve. When we are engaged in the service of our fellowmen, not only do our deeds assist them, but we put our own problems in a fresher perspective. When we concern ourselves more with others, there is less time to be concerned with ourselves! In the midst of the miracle of serving, there is the promise of Jesus that by losing ourselves, we find ourselves! ("President Kimball Speaks Out on Service to Others," *New Era*, March 1981)

Our extraordinary elder learned how to serve and love others by serving. President Kimball continued,

> The abundant life noted in the scriptures is the spiritual sum that is arrived at by the multiplying of our service to others and by investing our talents in service to God and to man. . . . In serving others, we "find" ourselves in terms of acknowledging divine guidance in our lives. Furthermore, the more we serve our fellowmen in appropriate ways, the more substance there is to our souls. We become more significant individuals as we serve others. We become more

> substantive as we serve others—indeed, it is easier to "find" ourselves because there is so much more of us to find! (Ibid.)

By the end of his mission, the fore mentioned missionary had served and loved as the Savior and had truly found himself. In our exit interview he said, "I love these people and don't want my mission to end. They are in my heart. My love and gratitude for Heavenly Father and His goodness has multiplied many fold. I'm so thankful for my mission experience. I will always be grateful to God for the Chilean people. I can and will love and serve God all the rest of my life and will never be able to repay Him for this wonderful chapter of my life." This was one of the many sweet experiences in my service to and with the missionaries of the Chile Santiago North Mission. I echo the feelings of the elder. I too am grateful for the blessing of our opportunity to serve, and I love our 563 missionaries and the people there.

In my own path of finding myself as I learn to trust the Lord and serve Him, I've had a special teacher who has taught me about service. This writing is the first time I've been so transparent, and in some ways, it shames me to confess my journey.

As previously shared, we were blessed with a special needs child. She is our first child, and from the moment her first cry filled the delivery room to this moment, I have always loved her. However, twenty-six doctors spanning nearly twelve years of trying to find out why she was not normal extracted a price of how much I liked being Chantel's parent. It was not what I had envisioned of parenthood and raising a family. Early on she cried a lot. She was a disruption in Church, and I detested the looks she got in social settings. Looking back, I took these things personally. I loved her with all my heart, but she was an interruption in my vision and expectation for a perfect life. I wanted the best for her, but I also wanted it for me. I had spurts of frustration because this was not something I could fix or control. I could see it was something I'd have to live with. For some time, I could say the right things and even believe that Chantel was to be and become one of our greatest blessings, but I was not enjoying the journey.

Then something happened to my heart. Heavenly Father answered my prayers with sending my wife to see her twin sister living in Germany. It was a nice break for her in her constant care of Chantel. I worked at home and would take the role of full-time caretaker while my wife was away for a couple of weeks. In the act of serving, feeding, and caring for her, there came a moment when I saw her differently. My heart was radically transformed. While I cannot pinpoint a particular act of service or specific deed, I do recall the moment and place in our Florida home when I had a paradigm shift and it all changed. Grace and the goodness of Jesus Christ brought a level of peace and a new love to my soul. Frustration turned to contentment. Anger turned to gratitude and delight. Despise for her circumstance turned to adoration and respect. I am so grateful for Chantel. I'm even more thankful for the grace that turned my heart and helped me to see things as they really are. There is a new level of love and gratitude for the blessing of being the parent of a special, even celestial, child. My sense of devotion to Father in Heaven has increased while the little service I can give to her is counted as one of the great blessings of my life.

## Self-Examination for Greater Gratitude

1. Is there a need in your life to elevate the level of your devotion and gratitude to God through finding miracles in giving service to others?
2. Have you had any experiences in your own journey that you need to write down or share with others?
3. Is there someone who you feel could benefit from becoming

more engaged in service? Can you share with them your feelings and an invitation to change?

## Scriptures for Consideration and Marking

1 Kings 17:7–16
Mosiah 2:17
Mosiah 2:20
Mosiah 24:14–16, 21
Alma 7:14

## Parting Thought

King Benjamin declared, "I tell you these things that ye may learn wisdom; that ye may learn that when ye are in the service of your fellow beings ye are only in the service of your God" (Mosiah 2:17). Let's look at Elder Perry's thought and invitation from the opening quote: "In our hearts do we feel a sense of gratitude and devotion to the Father? Are we of one heart with Him to whom we owe everything? The test of our devotion to the Lord seems to be the way we serve Him." A thankful heart is evidenced by how well we serve Him by serving those around us.

# 22

# Thank the Creator

"How much better it would be if all could be more aware of God's providence and love and express that gratitude to Him. . . . Our degree of gratitude is a measure of our love for Him. . . . Think of our physical sustenance. It is truly heaven-sent. The necessities of air, food, and water all come to us as gifts from a loving Heavenly Father. The earth was created to support our brief sojourn in mortality. We were born with a capacity to grow, love, marry, and form families." (Russell M. Nelson, "Thanks Be to God," *Ensign*, May 2012)

Within the last century one November night in Farmington, New Mexico, I took my first breath. Sometime later my eyes saw more than just light; they were able to focus on and recognize the facial images of my mother and others who cared for me. My ears could detect sounds, and I jumped at loud and abrupt noises. Imperceptibly without announcement, my taste buds developed, and I could differentiate between the sweet, soothing taste of Mother's milk, apple juice, mashed potatoes, or candy. I learned to detect the inviting smells of bacon, popcorn, and vanilla in contrast to repugnant odors that give us the urge to vomit. And so it goes—natural, progressive steps come as we develop. My heart has been beating thirty-six million times a year, and I breathe in and out approximately seven million times in the same period. I've learned to crawl, walk, run, climb, and so on. Human development is a beautiful manifestation of the genius and glory of our Creator. Every element of development is in its proper time and order. For most, we don't even think about, much less express, heartfelt gratitude to God for these blessings.

Once in a while due to accident, illness, or a fluke of nature, we lose one or more of these tender mercies that come with being born into the human family. It is then we suddenly become aware and grateful. Many of us have had an experience of losing capacity to breathe, see, smell, hear, walk, or talk. As an athlete, I was put on the sidelines for an ankle sprain or muscle bruise. Typhoid fever shortened my mission in Mexico, and I became painfully aware of how the body can react to disease. Shortly after returning from our mission in Chile, I had a bout with shingles in my ear. Pain and swelling caused my ear canal to swell and close shut. I couldn't hear most of what was being said by others, and I felt, for a time, that I was in a cocoon. My equilibrium was affected and I frequently staggered, nearly falling as I got out of bed each day. The ringing in my ears was annoying and frustrating. It was then I became aware of the profound blessing of hearing and having healthy ears. I prayed for the blessing to return. The doctor told me on one of my visits that it was possible I could lose the hearing in one of my ears. My prayers became more intense, and I promised myself and the Lord that I'd never take for granted the gift of hearing. Since these blessings of sight, smell, hearing, and breathing are with us from almost the beginning of our lives, we are generally pretty complacent with them, as if it's our human entitlement. For a few weeks I became more aware of facial movement while others talked, trying to read the lips and eye expressions of those talking to me. Finally, I remember awaking to the sounds of dripping water and the deep breathing of my sleeping wife. It was a beautiful moment. I immediately rolled out of bed on my knees and thanked Heavenly Father for the return of this profoundly special sense I had previously taken for granted. My hearing returned 100 percent.

Elder Nelson taught,

> Each organ of your body is a wondrous gift from God. Each eye has an autofocusing lens. Nerves and muscles control two eyes to make a single three-dimensional image. The eyes are connected to the brain, which records the sights seen.
>
> Your heart is an incredible pump. It has four delicate valves that control the direction of blood flow. These valves open and close more than 100,000 times a day—36 million times a year. Yet, unless altered by disease, they are able to withstand such stress almost indefinitely.
>
> Think of the body's defense system. To protect it from harm, it perceives pain. In response to infection, it generates antibodies. The skin provides protection. It warns against injury that excessive heat or cold might cause.
>
> The body renews its own outdated cells and regulates the levels of its own vital ingredients. The body heals its cuts, bruises, and broken bones. Its capacity for reproduction is another sacred gift from God. (Ibid.)

The interchange and experience of Alma and Korihor provides interesting insight. Korihor was an anti-Christ who sought to challenge Alma in his testimony. In Alma 30:43–48, Korihor challenged Alma to give him a sign as evidence there really was a God. In verses 49–52, Alma responded by calling down the powers of heaven to provide a sign to this man who was causing so much trouble among the people.

When Korihor could not speak, he realized he'd always had a testimony of the divinity of God and the blessings he too was born with. His hardened heart was touched with evidence too late. His life tragically ended as the prideful Zoramite apostates trampled and trodden him to death (Alma 30:59–60).

Helen Keller said Anne Sullivan taught her that "the best and most beautiful things in the world cannot be seen nor even touched, but just felt in the heart" (*Quote Investigator*, http://

quoteinvestigator.com/2012/07/18/best-not-seen/). Though no one reading this will be in the same category as Korihor (an anti-Christ or unbeliever), we can have memory loss and become forgetful of the wonder of blessings and tender mercies given by our Creator.

## Self-Examination for Greater Gratitude

1. As you consider the gifts of sight, smell, sound, and taste, as well as the motor skills of walking and running, are you grateful? How can you become more aware of those blessings without having to lose one or more of them?
2. What can you do to impress and teach others to be more gratefully aware of these blessings?
3. Is it time to write in your journal or to vocally express to others your appreciation for these profound blessings often taken for granted? When and how will you do it?

## Scriptures for Consideration and Marking

Alma 30:43–52
Alma 30:59–60
D&C 78:19
Hebrews 13:15
Psalm 105:1
Psalm 106:1

## Parting Thought

When you open the drapes and greet the morning sun shining through the window, be inclined to say, "Thank you, Father, for the sun and the light and warmth it provides." We do not own those blessings. We must find a way to become more aware and to possess a more thankful heart for God's gifts we so often take for granted. When you find a way, share it.

# 23

# *Becoming Grateful*

"Simple, rejuvenating experiences surround us. They can be safety valves to keep the tension down and the spirit up. Don't concentrate on what you don't have or have lost. . . . Select something like music, dance, sculpture, or poetry. Being creative will help you enjoy life. It engenders a spirit of gratitude. It develops latent talent, sharpens your capacity to reason, to act, and to find purpose in life. It dispels loneliness and heartache. It gives a renewal, a spark of enthusiasm, and zest for life." (Richard G. Scott, "Finding Joy in Life," *Ensign*, May 1996)

We've all watched the drama of a movie or a television series in which some crime has been committed and skilled detectives work to solve the case of who is responsible for the offense against the law. Forensic specialists trained in the investigative process search to find evidence that will identify suspects. They look for informational patterns in an effort to find supporting proof to indict a criminal and bring them to justice.

On the other hand, those perpetrating the crime against others strategize how to cover their tracks and maintain images and circumstances that support their innocence. They seek to mask the truth and maintain a blanket of evidence that keeps them clear of any wrongdoing.

And so it goes, a game between investigators and perpetrators to either bring criminals to justice or to maintain innocence while they carry on their evil offenses. One of the first and key markers in an investigation includes fingerprints. Criminals wear gloves or sometimes try to erase their prints, and investigators dust for even the slightest touching of anything near or associated with the crime scene. They know a fingerprint on a glass, a weapon, or anywhere in the proximity matched with a suspect can eliminate some suspects and raise the level of probability in others. Yes, fingerprints are key evidence to condemn the guilty or acquit the innocent. These markers are important in bringing closure to cases when they can be found.

I propose that our Creator is both busy and anxious to leave His fingerprints all over His creations to give evidence that He loves His children and desires to bless them. He makes no effort to cover up or conceal His involvement in all that is good. On the other hand, we, His children, can miss or be blinded to the rather obvious evidences that will truly convict Him of all that is good. The fingerprints of a loving Father in Heaven and His Son, our Savior and Redeemer are on all things.

At age one, as I toddled about our home, I had the misfortune of falling forward and placing my hands on a hot coal stove. After precious moments, the tender flesh of my one-year-old hands was literally cooked and was so profound that much of the flesh remained on the stove when my hands were finally taken from the stove. The severity of the burns produced a prognosis and recommendation from the doctor that my hands were to be removed surgically. There was no known way to save them. "They will always be useless appendages with zero functionality, and the risk of infection and other problems make us believe that amputation is the best option at this point," the doctor said. But mother knew of greater power than the wisdom gained in a medical school. My father, attended by my grandfathers, gave me a priesthood blessing.

In time, my hands were preserved, and they are perfectly functional, although they bear large wax-like scars on my palms. Mother agonized, and every time she saw or thought of my scars, she lamented and convicted herself of not being watchful or sufficiently attentive. In one visit with her just prior to her passing, she took my hands in hers and with a tear in her eye said, "Oh David, I am so sorry you've had to live your life with these scars. I should have been more alert and mindful. Will you please forgive me?"

I looked at my hands and replied, "Mother, I like my scars. They are reminders and visible evidence of an important miracle in my life and are tokens to remind me of the importance of God and His goodness and mercy." Additionally, I was taught over the years that the greatest miracles are not the healing of sick bodies but rather the healing of broken hearts and spiritual ailment.

Look for the evidences to build the case of the grand truth that God is our Heavenly Father and He loves us. Assemble the markers and every validation to convict and support the fact that Jesus Christ is indeed our Savior and Redeemer, as well as Creator and Exemplar. Some of the most visible fingerprints are in His creations. Let's not get so busy or distracted that we miss catching the most obvious identifying markers of His love.

Elder Scott adds,

> Do you take time to discover each day how beautiful your life can be? How long has it been since you watched the sun set? The departing rays kissing the clouds, trees, hills, and lowlands good night, sometimes tranquilly, sometimes with exuberant bursts of color and form. What of the wonder of a cloudless night when the Lord unveils the marvels of His heavens—the twinkling stars, the moonlight rays—to ignite our imagination with His greatness and glory? How captivating to watch a seed planted in fertile soil germinate, gather strength, and send forth a tiny, seemingly insignificant sprout. Patiently it begins to grow and develop its own character led by the genetic code the Lord has provided to guide its development. . . . You are one of the noblest of

> God's creations. His intent is that your life be gloriously beautiful regardless of your circumstances. As you are grateful and obedient, you can become all that God intends you to be. (Ibid.)

Let's look not only at His creations, which truly testify of Him, but also at His healing hands, which mend burned hands and broken hearts. His fingerprints evidence that repentance is one of the first principles of the gospel and really does offer peace to the soul, a rebirth, change, and a new heart. Let's watch for the spark of divinity that lights up in many of His children as they forgive others, help the needy, show patience, exhibit charity, and emulate His other attributes.

May we be extraordinary in our investigations and observations in identifying the fingerprints, divine signatures, and tender mercies of our Father in Heaven and our Savior. They are everywhere. May it develop a more thankful heart in all of us.

**Self-Examination for Greater Gratitude**

1. Do you take time to observe and enjoy His creations? What will you do to be more keen in developing the capacity to be watchful?
2. Stop your busyness for an hour each week and add to a list of fingerprints you've noticed during the week. Review the list and stay aware of His involvement in your life.
3. Who in your life needs to adjust their view and develop a more thankful heart by noting the goodness of God, His Son, and the Holy Ghost? Find a way to share with them.

**Scriptures for Consideration and Marking**

2 Nephi 4:17–28
Psalm 95:2
Psalm 147:7
1 Corinthians 11:24

## Parting Thought

Heavenly Father will bless you in your desire to increase and maintain an awareness of His hand in your life. As we make time and search for ways to remember our blessings, He will help us remember. President Marion G. Romney once said, "I bear my testimony to you that the Lord wants us to be grateful and thankful unto him. And if we do these things which he has advised us to do, we will be the happiest people who dwell upon the earth, for this is the way to the presence and society of our Father in heaven" (Marion G. Romney, "Gratitude and Thanksgiving," *Ensign*, November 1982). What a wonderful insight and attendant promise!

# 24

# Enjoy Your Blessings Now

"If we constantly focus only on the stones in our mortal path, we will almost surely miss the beautiful flower or cool stream provided by the loving Father who outlined our journey. Each day can bring more joy than sorrow when our mortal and spiritual eyes are open to God's goodness. Joy in the gospel is not something that begins only in the next life. It is our privilege now, this very day. We must never allow our burdens to obscure our blessings. There will always be more blessings than burdens—even if some days it doesn't seem so. Jesus said, 'I am come that they might have life, and that they might have it more abundantly.' Enjoy those blessings right now. They are yours and always will be." (Jeffrey R. Holland, "What I Wish Every New Member Knew—and Every Longtime Member Remembered," *Ensign*, October 2006)

There are a couple of terrible human diseases that torment and challenge humankind. One is called Excusitis and the other is "If I had, then I could" syndrome. While neither is fatal, both can surely retard growth and spoil one's life. The symptoms are rather easy to detect in others but sometimes a little tough to diagnose in oneself.

Excusitis is characterized by statements like "I didn't accomplish this because . . ." or "I would have, but I couldn't because . . ." or "I can't because of . . ." Those with Excusitis always have a seemingly bona fide excuse for everything. There is always a reason why they are unable to accomplish or attain desirable results. We all know someone plagued with this disease.

I knew a person who felt he couldn't be happy because his father left his mother for another and that ruined everything. He was understandably disappointed in his father for the choices he had made; yet he allowed the situation to set a roadblock in his own progression and enjoyment. He brought up the subject frequently in a variety of circumstances. "I won't ever be the same because of what Dad did." He planned to get his university education from an Ivy League or other prestigious school but often said, "My dad promised to help me finance my education, but he really messed up the dream when he started roaming." When it came time to serve a mission, his excuse was that he needed to stay home to help his mother work through her problems. Relating to his work, he said, "I think I could have been promoted more in my work, but this whole thing with my dad has made me less motivated." He struggled in his marriage, saying things like, "I have a hard time trusting others, which I think comes from my dad's stupidity." He had an excuse at every turn.

Others can't enjoy living because they are too short, too tall, too fat, or not smart enough. Some can't have joy in the moment because the rules are too restrictive or the pay too low. We can find these folks all around us. They can't succeed or have joy because of some excuse.

Those with the "If I had, then I could" syndrome likewise struggle to find joy in the journey of life because there's always something they are missing. You can hear them say, "If I just had a new computer, then I'd be more successful" or "If I had an extra savings cushion of maybe $10,000, then I'd feel a lot more in control of my circumstances." Some might say, "If I had been called to a foreign mission instead of Boise, I think I would have been a better missionary" or "If I just had another companion, then I'd be much more content in my mission experience." Sadly, in today's world too many say, "If I just had a different spouse, then I'd be happy" or "If my parents would let me have a cell phone, then I'd really be happy" or even "If my children were more focused in their education, then I'd feel a lot better about their lives."

If the weather were nicer, if the neighbors were more friendly, if I could lose ten pounds, if she just wouldn't do that, if he would just work harder—there's always something in the equation that's missing. Joy, enjoyment, happiness, and fun are always a step or two away due to something we don't have. The constant conditional statement, spoken or simply thought, "If I had, then I could" keeps many from the joy Father in Heaven wants us all to feel now. We don't have to wait until everything is perfect to have joy in our journey.

The interesting thing about both of these diseases is that there is never a shortage for excuses, and when those inflicted with "If I had, then I could" syndrome get what they want, there is always something else to take its place. In both there is a complete absence of gratitude and a feeling that leads toward complaint or murmuring. To answer the question "Why am I less than what I should be?" people only have a few options. They can self-examine in the spirit of personal responsibility, or they can find an excuse of something they don't yet have that could fix their problem. Elder Holland taught in another conference talk, "No misfortune is so bad that whining about it won't make it worse" (Jeffrey R. Holland, "The Tongue of Angels," *Ensign*, May 2007).

One of the best and most effective ways to cure both of these anomalies is to follow the Savior's admonition to "be of good cheer. . . . [T]he blessings thereof are yours, and the riches of eternity are yours" (D&C 78:18; see also verse 7). After all, the Savior speaks from experience with bad days when things did not go well. He knew something about others challenging His position and declaration of lineage. Still, in His progression and perfection, He did not make excuses, nor did He complain that He would have been happier if things were different. Instead He loved, healed, lifted, and befriended. He was optimistic, happy, and always complimentary of His Father. In every down day, He trusted in the will of His Father.

We can learn to be likewise—happy in our challenges; trusting in the Father's will; optimistic in knowing that the Father, His Son, and the Holy Ghost will work together to provide for our success. No excuses and no "If I had, then I could" mentality.

### Self-Examination for Greater Gratitude

1. In a spirit of self-responsibility, looking at your own life, do you see any tendencies toward Excusitis or "If I had, then I could" syndrome? If so, what will you do to check it and move toward cheerful gratitude?
2. If you haven't already done it, make a list of all the things you've been blessed with and count all the reasons you have to "be of good cheer."
3. Help someone you know with one of the two diseases get cured. Teach them in a fun and positive way about Excusitis and the "If I had, then I could" syndrome. Challenge them to become aware of the diseases, and check yourself.

### Scriptures of Consideration and Marking

D&C 78:17–18
Luke 22:17
D&C 117:7
Mark 8:6
Philippians 4:6

### Parting Thought

Elder Holland refers to Orson F. Whitney's teaching that "the spirit of the gospel is optimistic; it trusts in God and looks on the bright side of things. The opposite or pessimistic spirit drags men down and away from God, looks on the dark side, murmurs, complains, and is slow to yield obedience." Elder Holland further counseled, "We should honor the Savior's declaration to 'be of good cheer.' (Indeed, it seems to me we may be more guilty of breaking that commandment than almost any other!)" (Jeffrey R. Holland, "The Tongue of Angels," *Ensign*, May 2007).

# 25

# Refinement and Stature

"A grateful heart will give you a touch of refinement that will come in no other way. . . . 'Thank you' is a wonderful phrase. Use it. It will add stature to your soul. Never let a day go by without saying thank you to someone for something—and especially to your Heavenly Father." (Marjorie Pay Hinckley, *Small and Simple Things* [Salt Lake City: Deseret Book, 2003] 12)

Vivid in my mind is an experience I had several years ago. While it was not a ward activity, it was nonetheless a tradition among some members of our Arizona ward to go to Rocky Point, Mexico, each Memorial Day weekend and enjoy the sand and surf of the Gulf of California. Many times, ten or fifteen families would make the round-trip five-hundred-mile pilgrimage from Gilbert, Arizona, to Puerto Penansco. Fresh shrimp was plentiful, and each family loaded their motor homes with enough food to feed five thousand—hamburgers, potato chips, and snacks galore. The safe, shallow ocean water provided a wonderful playground for the younger children, while the teens and their dads rode ATVs and played an occasional game of football. Sunday included Church services and more low-key activities for the day. It was a great time for all, and many memories were created there as we played, ate, sang, soaked up the sun, and had a good time. It was a special treat for me to be around the people of Mexico. I served my mission in that wonderful country, and there is forever a special place in my heart for them.

One evening about sunset, two or three families barbequed hamburgers on the grill and set out all the chips, snacks, potato salad, shrimp, and so on. Off a short distance from the crowd, an older Mexican man sat next to a large piece of driftwood. He was looking out into the gulf at the setting sun. Even from the distance you could see his sun-wrinkled face; unshaven beard of a week or more; tattered, well-worn clothing; and tire-tread sandals on his feet. As I sat and observed him watching the sun dip, I couldn't help but feel the contrast in our lives. I wondered what he was thinking. Did he have a family? Where did he work to provide for himself? There I sat in my comfort, with a full stomach and a good life. I wondered about his.

I was so focused on him that I was surprised when I saw a small boy from one of the families in our group walking toward him with a plate of food heaped to overflowing. A few chips and Cheetos marked the path from the group to the old man with his head turned to the sunset. When the little boy was ten feet or so from the man, an unthinking father called out, "Hey, don't give him that. He will stick with us the whole time we're here." Now we were all looking on. The boy called back to his dad, "But he's hungry!" No one spoke, and the dad, now embarrassed by the unfolding situation, also watched without further comment. The old Mexican man had turned toward the boy and was engaged in what was happening. A few more chips fell to the ground as the little boy dropped to his knees. Kneeling in front of the man, the boy reached out and handed him the plate. I wish I could have a photograph of those two faces looking at each other, just after sundown on a beach in Mexico. The boy with innocent love in his eyes, and the old man looking at him with a near-toothless grateful smile. One giving, and the other receiving, while a grateful bishop and a portion of his flock looked on in one of the greatest unplanned teaching moments ever. The old man looked at the boy, nodded with gratitude, and said, "Gracias." To complete his task, the boy ran back to the food table to retrieve a can of soda pop and a half dozen cookies. From the old man there was again a nod of gratitude and an audible "gracias."

There are many takeaways from that experience. One is the perception of a child and his desire to share, as well as the graciousness and dignity of the old man who said thank you with the look in his eyes and with the spoken word. Sister Hinckley's insight from the beginning quote comes to mind again: "A grateful heart will give you a touch of refinement that will come in no other way. . . . 'Thank you' is a wonderful phrase. Use it. It will add stature to your soul." The group of ward members, including the embarrassed father and a dozen other onlooking spectators, were indeed students who were also grateful for what happened there that day.

Saying thank you truly does add to the stature of the soul. It's something I've noticed in Honduras and Ghana when people shake your hand, look into your eyes, and say, "Thank you for what you are doing for the people in our country." I've seen it when students makes their way to the front of a seminary or institute classroom and say to their teacher, "Thank you for today's lesson. What you said answered my constant prayer." I've seen it when a mother opens a little note from her son and reads, "Thank you, Mom. You are the best!" I've seen it when employees approach their employer and say, "Thank you for the opportunity to work here. I hope I am making a contribution, because I really value what our product can do for consumers. Thank you!" A thankful heart expresses with action and word "Thank you!"

**Self-Examination for Greater Gratitude**

1. Who do you need to say thank you to? Make a list and set a plan to do so.
2. How can you develop the habit of expressing thanks every day for simple acts of love or exhibition of discipleship to Christ? List and make a plan.

3. Take some time and write in your journal of people in your life who have made a difference by saying thank you.

## Scriptures for Consideration and Marking

Daniel 1:6–21
D&C 89:11
Matthew 26:27
Alma 61:2–9
Psalm 106:1

## Parting Thought

Sister Hinckley had a touch of common sense about her that was fun and affectionate. Regarding this subject of saying thank you, she offers the following delightful counsel: "And when you finally develop a little gratitude in your heart, make up your mind to express it. 'Appreciation unexpressed is not appreciation.' If you can't find someone to say thank you to for something, just take a look at your toothbrush and say, 'Thank you for being. You are a wonderful little gadget' " (*Glimpses into the Life and Heart of Marjorie Pay Hinckley*, edited by Virginia H. Pearce [Salt Lake City: Deseret Book, 1999]). May we develop a more expressive thankful heart that is no stranger to "Thank you," "I appreciate," "I'm glad I know you," and "I am grateful to God for your goodness and example."

# 26

# Blessings in Hardships

"When we give thanks in all things, we see hardships and adversities in the context of the purpose of life. We are sent here to be tested. There must be opposition in all things. We are meant to learn and grow through that opposition, through meeting our challenges, and through teaching others to do the same. . . . The Lord will not only consecrate our afflictions for our gain, but He will use them to bless the lives of countless others." (Dallin H. Oaks, "Give Thanks in All Things," *Ensign,* May 2003)

Why do some people have so many challenges in life? What is the place of opposition and adversity? Is it possible that prosperity and affluence are actually the most difficult forms of adversity to identify and ultimately overcome? Why does earth life have so many thorns, thistles, and harmful spiny weeds, and how does a person deal with the required sweat, toil, and endless labor?

Sometimes the answers to the above questions are simple. Lots of challenges come from our own poor or incorrect choices. Others are a direct result of the agency of others who make unrighteous choices themselves or impose their domination and control upon us. Whatever the case, opposition was introduced as a fundamental constant in Heavenly Father's plan. Agency and the right to choose combined with opposition and adversity are foundational in the earthly portion of our path to eternal life.

I know a righteous family who sought a blessing from Elder LeGrand Richards years ago. Their faith-filled daughter in her thirties—then married to a good and righteous man and a mother of three—had been impacted two decades earlier by a crippling disease. She knew if faith could move mountains, then hers was sufficient to ask the Lord to heal her. An appointment was made, and a special family fast and temple session preceded the appointment. As Elder Richards counseled with the family prior to the blessing, he was prompted to teach the family and their daughter an important principle. He taught that the adversity of her condition was one of the reasons the family had been so blessed. The challenges, in fact, had played a critical role in educating the entire family and increasing their faith and testimony. It was almost as if he taught "this life is such a short part of eternity and this situation is in fact a crowning jewel, a wonderful blessing, and an answer to the pleadings of two parents asking that their children become strong and stay faithful to the end."

Because we have so much in common, my sweetheart and I know of several other couples who have been blessed, as we have, to be caregivers of some of Heavenly Father's most valiant spirits—disabled spiritual giants who live their earthy life with special needs. One dominant question we all have is, "What happens if our special, even celestial, children outlive us? Will they become a burden, instead of a blessing, to someone else? Will others care for our child with the same joy and gladness?"

In other situations, some have lost their employment and struggled to find new work to support their families. In some cases, after lengthy periods of unemployment, they have to make major and even drastic relocation moves to secure new jobs. For many it was challenging for their children to change schools, find new friends with high standards, and transition in other ways. However, most have said as they look in the rearview mirror a few years later, "That was a really important time in the growth, testimony building, and unification of our family." Others will say, "What a blessing that was to one particular child in our home." Yet others will report, "We had to move halfway across the country for one of our children to find their eternal companion. She's worth it!"

We are acquainted with others who feel embarrassed and helpless for children who have made wrong choices. Others have been visited by a tragic death and feel the loss of a child, spouse, or other loved one. Still others are challenged by feelings of rejection and a severe loss that accompanies divorce.

Sometimes we think of adversity as economic challenges, health issues, or broken hearts. We yearn and pray for prosperity and sometimes feel that if we can have our economic adversities removed we will be free from opposition. But could it be that even prosperity serves as an opposition and challenge to some? While this kind of adversity could appear to be more palatable or even fun, the end result can be more spiritually damaging than broken bones or empty bank accounts. I was once taught that every age of man has had it's adversity and challenge to test faith and trust in God. For each era in the timeline of earth, it came in different forms. Adam had his challenges, and Abraham his. The early Saints had theirs, and so did those who lived through a world depression. For some in our day, it comes in the form of abundance and prosperity. Many of us have so much, even too much. How will we handle our adversity of abundance?

One of my favorite quotes is by Orson F. Whitney:

> No pain that we suffer, no trial that we experience is wasted. It ministers to our education, to the development of such qualities as patience, faith, fortitude, and humility. All that we suffer . . . builds up our character, purifies our hearts, expands our soul, and makes us more tender and charitable, more worthy to be called the children of God . . . and it is through sorrow and suffering, toil and tribulation, that we gain the education which will make us more like our Father

> and Mother in Heaven. (Quoted in Spencer W. Kimball, *Faith Precedes the Miracle* [Salt Lake City: Deseret Book, 2001), 98)

The Mormon pioneers reported how their adversities were a price they paid to be blessed with greater testimony of the love of God. I am inspired by their insightful perspective:

> I have pulled my handcart when I was so weak and weary from illness and lack of food that I could hardly put one foot ahead of the other. I have looked ahead and seen a patch of sand or a hill slope and I have said I can go only that far and there I must give up for I cannot pull the load through it. . . . I have gone on to that sand and when I reached it the cart began pushing me. I have looked back many times to see who was pushing my cart, but my eyes saw no one. I knew then that the angels of God were there. The price we paid to become acquainted with God was a privilege to pay. (Francis Webster, *Martin Handcart Company, Relief Society Magazine,* January 1948, 8)

One of my great personal heroes is a man whose life was envied by many. He has a Harvard MBA, was a chief financial officer for several major corporations, ran marathons, served as bishop and in a stake presidency, and above all else is a great family man. Unpredictably his health collapsed, and he's spent the past several years in and out of hospitals. He had a liver transplant that brings its own challenges, has seen his financial position change dramatically, lost much of his capacity to serve in the Church, and is currently facing the probable amputation of his leg. He's been close to being transferred from this world several times. With all these challenges and adversity, he recently testified to me, "I am experiencing new opportunities to do things that I never would have had if I had all my health back. My understanding of the Atonement has been expanded from seeing it only as a solution for sin and spiritual illness. I've gained deeper understanding of its power to comfort and ease our physical burdens and sufferings, as well. With all my challenges, 99.9 percent of the population of the world would trade places with me in a New York minute. I have a strong testimony, the gospel, an extraordinary wife, four wonderful children, and thirteen grandchildren. I am a very blessed man." He then shared a poem by an unknown author:

Dear God,
I didn't sleep well last night, but I did wake up.
My muscles are sore, but they work.
My wallet is not full, but my belly is.
I may not have all I want, but I have all I need.
My life is not perfect, but my life is good.
—Jesse Joseph (quoted in Manny Garcia, "Seeking a Deeper Walk," *Bangor Liberty Friends Church*, http://www.blfchurch.org/bell/archive/2014/bell2014-11.htm)

Neal A. Maxwell added his testimony, "Now, as you and I look at our lives . . . we sometimes do not understand that through which we are passing, but, being submissive, we can trust Him. The day will come, brothers and sisters, when the tapestry of your life will be unfolded, and you will see divine design all through it, and praise God for the experience and the tutoring which, in His goodness, He has given you" (Elder Neal A. Maxwell, BYU–Hawaii Devotional, 9 February 1988).

## Self-Examination for Greater Gratitude

1. In your own adversities and challenges, can you see blessings and opportunities for growth? Have you recorded the things you've learned in your journal?

2. How can you teach your family the important principles contained in Elder Oaks's teachings about the value and place of adversity in our lives?
3. Who do you know who is struggling and challenged by something? What can you do to help them understand the role of opposition in their lives?

## Scriptures for Consideration and Marking

| | |
|---|---|
| Mosiah 26:38–39 | 1 Thessalonians 5:18 |
| Alma 37:37 | D&C 78:19 |
| 2 Nephi 2:1–2 | 2 Corinthians 12:7–10 |

## Parting Thought

Consider an additional teaching from Elder Oaks: "When we understand this principle, that God offers us opportunities for blessings and blesses us through our own adversities and the adversities of others, we can understand why He has commanded us again and again to 'thank the Lord thy God in all things'" (Dallin H. Oaks, "Give Thanks in All Things," *Ensign,* May 2003). Yes, from the beginning, agency and opposition have always been part of the plan of Heavenly Father. The key to how we handle whatever ways our adversity and opposition appear is the level of our heartfelt trust in God, knowing that His ways are not always our ways.

# 27

# Happiness

"I am confident that we can attain the happiness we desire and that God wants for us. It is my prayer that as we pursue the true path to happiness in our families and professions, we will use our knowledge and influence to bring greater righteousness, peace, understanding, and freedom to people all over the world. I assure you that the joy, love, and fulfillment experienced in loving, righteous families produce the greatest possible happiness we can achieve." (Quentin L. Cook, "The True Path to Happiness," *Ensign*, June 2011)

It has been said that the greatest of joys and the deepest of sorrows are found within the family circle. There is nothing that brings more joy to parents' hearts than seeing their children living happy and fulfilling lives. There are few things more important to a child than to be able to say, "I have the greatest parents in the world. I know they love me and would do about anything for me." Few things are more fulfilling than being in a marriage where each spouse feels adored by the other and is totally faithful and loyal. We should cherish, be grateful for, and freely express our thankful hearts to God and others for these blessings.

We can also see that great sorrow comes to parents when they see their children sad, depressed, or making self-destructing choices. There are few things that stab at the heart with more penetrating grief and personal rejection than for children to see one of their parents reject, abuse, violate, or abandon their other parent. Deep distress and suffering come from having one of their parents violate marriage covenants and leave the family emotionally and economically in limbo, if not completely destitute.

Sorrow and feelings of hopelessness are not reserved only for those who have challenges in family matters. Let's briefly consider one of Lucifer's more effective tools of our times—depression. While I don't pretend to understand it, I know it's real. I have observed its destructive power. I know that wonderful, worthy, and able disciples of Christ are paralyzed by not having a sense of self-worth, not feeling fulfilled or deserving of happiness. Satan somehow makes good people feel less positively about themselves when they get consumed by comparing themselves at their worst with others at their best. Competition has a high potential for the birthing of the universal sin of pride, but comparison of our faults with others' virtues is unfair, to say the least. Satan inserts his spoiling influence when he creates discontent with parenthood, feeling overwhelmed with duties and expectations of being the physical and emotional provider. He attacks the one thing he can never have—a body. He makes us feel deficient by being too skinny or too fat, inappropriately short or awkwardly tall, or too bald or grey or ugly.

The depressed seem to grovel in a web of discouragement, drowning in a pool of hopelessness and paralyzed by self-deception.

For a non-professional without proper training and education in the matter, it is inappropriate for me to suggest a solution to this cross some have to bear. As a priesthood leader, I have found the majority of those depressed seem to find the seeds of their challenges in the matters of family, educational pursuit, and profession. Because of my chapters working with missionaries, I have also seen it in the righteous desires of young missionaries who compare themselves with Ammon in the Book of Mormon, Paul in the New Testament, or Wilford Woodruff in the latter days bringing masses to the truth of the gospel.

In his October 2013 general conference address, Elder Jeffrey R. Holland taught, "The Book of Mormon says Ammon and his brethren were depressed at a very difficult time, and so can the rest of us be. But today I am speaking of something more serious, of an affliction so severe that it significantly restricts a person's ability to function fully, a crater in the mind so deep that no one can responsibly suggest it would surely go away if those victims would just square their shoulders and think more positively—though I am a vigorous advocate of square shoulders and positive thinking!" (Jeffrey R. Holland, "Like a Broken Vessel," *Ensign*, November 2013). Elder Holland provided insight and encouragement, and if you know someone who is challenged by depression, I recommend that you read and reread the talk.

He gave the following counsel and encouragement that correlates appropriately with Elder Cook's message in our key quote for the day. Elder Holland reminded us, "I testify of the holy Resurrection, that unspeakable cornerstone gift in the Atonement of the Lord Jesus Christ! With the Apostle Paul, I testify that that which was sown in corruption will one day be raised in incorruption and that which was sown in weakness will ultimately be raised in power. . . . Until that hour when Christ's consummate gift is evident to us all, may we live by faith, hold fast to hope, and show 'compassion one of another' " (ibid.).

The Prophet Joseph Smith taught: "Happiness is the object and design of our existence; and will be the end thereof, if we pursue the path that leads to it; and this path is virtue, uprightness, faithfulness, holiness, and keeping all the commandments of God" (Joseph Smith, *Teachings of the Prophet Joseph Smith*, selected by Joseph Fielding Smith [Salt Lake City: Deseret Book, 1976], 255). In the end, our pursuit of happiness begins, continues, and ends in the path that goes through the family circle. Happy and thankful hearts center on "joy, love, and fulfillment experienced in loving, righteous families" (Quentin L. Cook, "The True Path to Happiness," *Ensign*, June 2011).

I have been blessed to observe, up close and fairly personal, loved ones who have been challenged by the unexplainable dark clouds of depression. In some cases, I have seen the benefit of professional intervention, and with others, the miracle of medication. I have observed loving, kind, and patient companions or spouses in others. In my experience of all cases that have been remedied or stabilized, I have been grateful to see extraordinary examples seeking to keep the Lord's commandments and staying constant in their effort to do whatever it takes to maintain family matters. The love and support of family is critical. Gratitude for those closest is enough to carry the challenged through the storms.

## Self-Examination for Greater Gratitude

1. What are you doing to build a foundation of family relationships that will provide love and kindness in cloudy days?
2. Do you know someone who needs your listening ear and accepting heart? What will you do to reach out and help?
3. Perhaps your experience with these matters deserves a journal entry.

## Scriptures for Consideration and Marking

| | |
|---|---|
| 1 Corinthians 15:42–58 | 1 Peter 3:8 |
| 2 Nephi 4:17–28 | 1 Nephi 2:7 |

## Parting Thought

Elder Holland told of an experience he had as a young married man when his car broke down in Southern Utah. It happened in the first thirty-four miles of a long 2,600-mile journey to the Eastern United States. With a lot of toil and challenges, he pressed on. Frustrated and discouraged he finally figured out a way to get his family to their destination. Many years later, he drove past that precise place where his car broke down. He imagined he could see the young wife and children near the car and the young man walking toward the nearest town. I quote his words: "His shoulders seemed to be slumping a little, the weight of a young father's fear evident in his pace. . . . In that imaginary instant, I couldn't help calling out to him: "Don't give up, boy. Don't you quit. You keep walking. You keep trying. There is help and happiness ahead—a lot of it—30 years of it now, and still counting. You keep your chin up. It will be all right in the end. Trust God and believe in good things to come" (Jeffrey R. Holland, "'An High Priest of Good Things to Come,'" *Ensign*, November 1999).

# 28

# Save to Be Saved

[Referring to the story of how a woodsman saved a lost child] "How would you feel . . . toward the nameless woodsman had he saved your little son? Would there be any end to your gratitude? To sense this is to feel something of the gratitude our Father must feel toward any of us who saves one of his children. Such gratitude is a prize dearly to be won, for the Lord has said, 'If it so be that you should labor all your days in crying repentance unto this people, and bring, save it be one soul unto me, how great shall be your joy with him in the kingdom of my Father!' Even so, I might add, if that soul should be our own." (Boyd K. Packer, "Where Much Is Given, Much Is Required," *Ensign*, November 1974)

How do you put a value on a human soul? During one of the world's darkest periods in places like the slave castle of Ghana, Africa, and the cotton fields of the South, there was little value placed on human life. Hitler differentiated the valuation of souls based on race and ethnic status. Even today there are leaders and cultures that discount the value of human life. Sadly, there have been many judgmental glitches regarding this question of human value.

We know God's most prized creation and most valuable asset is His children—beyond the grandeur of the mountains, oceans, seas, snowfields, or sandy beaches. His joy is in their growth and goodness. Let's consider the story told by Elder Jacob de Jager in general conference. During a severe storm, a lifeboat was sent out to rescue the crew of a distressed fishing boat. They reached the ship, but the rowboat was too small and one man had to stay behind. The rescue crew was exhausted after making it back to the beach. The local coast guard captain asked the crowd gathered on the beach for volunteers to go back for the man left on the boat. When nineteen-year-old Hans stepped forward, his mother begged him not to go, saying that his father had died at sea and his brother Pete had been lost at sea for more than three months. Hans told his mother that he felt he had to do it and it was his duty. Elder de Jager relates of the incident:

> After a struggle with the high-going seas that lasted for more than an hour (and to Hans's mother it seemed an eternity), the rowboat came into sight again. When the rescuers had approached the beach close enough so that the captain of the coast guard could reach them by shouting, he cupped his hands around his mouth and called vigorously against the storm, "Did you save him?"
>
> And then the people lighting the sea with their torches saw Hans rise from his rowing bench, and he shouted with all his might, "Yes! And tell Mother it is my brother Pete!" (Jacob de Jager, "You Never Know Who You May Save," *Ensign*, November 1976)

What is the value of a soul? This is such an interesting question and has an obvious answer. Each is a child of God, offspring of Deity, with a potential of infinite possibilities to become like Heavenly Father and Mother and to eventually have all that He has. Incomprehensible as it is, we are nonetheless seeds of godhood. No wonder each soul has such value.

Recently my sweetheart and I traveled to the lands of our fathers in Europe (Scandinavia, England, and Italy). There with qualified historians, not only did we see where our ancestors were born, were christened, were married, and lived their lives, but we revisited the stories of their conversion to the gospel of Jesus Christ and subsequent immigration to Zion. We were reminded of the faith and sacrifice of Lorenzo Snow and his companions as they dedicated themselves to sharing the news of the Restoration. We became intensely appreciative of the missionaries who brought the gospel to our ancestors and began the change of religious understanding that has rippled through hundreds and thousands of decedents.

From our historian guide in Denmark, we listened to the stories of great-great-grandmother Dorthea and the hardships she endured through her life. The gospel brought her hope of brighter days. Although she turned her face to Zion, their poverty would only permit passage of one family member to America. My great-grandfather, William Otto Edward Thorwald, at age eleven was selected from her four children to be the first to go. She lived with hope that someday she and the other children could follow. It must have crossed her mind at least once or twice that when she said good-bye to her son with Brother John Forsgren, she'd never see him again. She finally made it to Salt Lake with the rest of the her children; she died just two years later at age forty-nine.

Our historian guide had studied her life in some detail and seemed to love her courage and fortitude. I remember his words: "Dorthea had a very, very hard life, and it's become my feeling that the purpose of her existence was to bear her children, find the restored gospel, and plant their feet in Zion." The worth of her soul has soared in my heart. I feel a great love for her for the value she placed on the souls of her four sons.

Similar stories are found on the maternal side of my pedigree. The change brought to my Waldensian ancestry and other families in the Piedmont valleys of Northern Italy was monumental when missionaries taught and baptized precious souls. From those converts have come thousands of descendents who have in turn served missions of their own in every corner of the planet. Bishops, stake presidents, mission presidents, temple presidents, and General Authorities bear those family names. The value of souls!

I am not a mathematician, but I love contemplating the mathematical fact that if you were to labor all your days to bring four souls to Christ in your eighty or so years on planet earth, and then each of those were to do the same—convert four souls—and likewise each of those were to be instruments to find and change four in each succeeding generation, the cumulative total in ten generations is 1,390,000 souls. Wow!

The Lord said, "And if it so be that you should labor all your days in crying repentance unto this people, and bring, save it be one soul unto me, how great shall be your joy with him in the kingdom of my Father! And now, if your joy will be great with one soul that you have brought unto me into the kingdom of my Father, how great will be your joy if you should bring many souls unto me!" (D&C 18:15–16)

## Self-Examination for Greater Gratitude

1. What are the stories of the first conversions in your family? Make sure your stories include the names of the missionaries and members who were key to the creating of your beginnings in the gospel.
2. Are you willing to find a way to thank the missionaries and members or their descendants for the gospel being in your life.
3. Make sure you journal not only the information but also your feelings.

## Scriptures for Consideration and Marking

D&C 18:15–16
John 4:36
Alma 29:113
James 5:19–20
Alma 26:11–16

## Parting Thought

Being grateful for those who have blessed us, as well as feeling gratitude to be an instrument in helping others, is important. Consideration of with whom and how we can share the gospel in the future is also important to the Lord. There is a scriptural message given by Paul that prompts a selfish reason for sharing the gospel. Paul wrote in the epistle to James, "Brethren, if any of you do err from the truth, and one convert him; let him know, that he which converteth the sinner from the error of his way shall save a soul from death, and shall hide a multitude of sins" (James 5:19–20). As a sinner, I can use the forgetfulness of my Judge when I bring souls unto Him. May we be grateful for the souls who saved us and, with a thankful heart, pass forward the blessings to other souls.

# 29
# Daughters of Eve

"As a Church, we have enormous respect and gratitude to you mothers of young children. We want you to be happy and successful in your families and to have the validation and support you need and deserve. . . . I hope all of you dear sisters, married or single, never wonder if you have worth in the sight of the Lord and to the leaders of the Church. We love you. We respect you and appreciate your influence in preserving the family and assisting with the growth and the spiritual vitality of the Church." (M. Russell Ballard, "Daughters of God," *Ensign,* May 2008)

With each passing chapter of my life I have an increasing love and appreciation for Eve. Temple teachings help me to see our first mother with grateful eyes and a thankful heart. Eve was amazing in her capacity to see things clearly and completely, and I have understood better her choice to partake of the fruit. I feel the same as I've watched my own "Eve" show the same capacity as Mother Eve to have a more complete and panoramic view of life. I've come to believe that we Adams are a lot like our Father Adam, who toil, labor, and execute, sometimes with a more narrow vision. We listen and seek to understand the parameters so that we can implement and administer, sometimes without seeing the whole picture. I have seen in our daughters something special as they take on their role (as defined by the proclamation on the family) with a different set of eyes and feelings than our sons.

Perhaps it's an overgeneralization, but I believe that Eves of all ages come equipped with special antennas for spiritual matters. This chapter is dedicated to celebrating the Eves of our lives, the women who bless us in so many ways. The following are a tiny sampling of many tributes given from boys and girls to Eves ages five to a hundred.

- My little sister is so sensitive. She puts little notes of encouragement in my sports shoes so that I find them when I'm preparing to play a game or run a race.
- Grandma has a unique ability to sense when I'm down or dealing with life stuff. She encourages me with little quotes that lift me and show her love and concern.
- Mother is nearly impossible to fool. She has this incredible ability to read between the lines, like really between the lines.
- There is something in my younger sister's psyche that prompts her to contact her social network of friends and ask them to write a note of encouragement to me. She does it for others too—sometimes people she hardly knows. I found out that when there was an untimely death in the family of one of our ward members, she engaged a blogger to reach out and make a difference with written words of solace and understanding. Those grieving were lifted.
- My grandma knows that life sails along pretty good when there is always a little candy in her special hiding place for grandkids. She has a toy room full of more toys than any of us can play with. It's like a treasure chest of hundreds of toys. Her dress-up room is full of clothes. We have so much fun dressing up for charades.
- Mom is the one I can be most transparent with. She always listens to get all the information she can before she reacts.
- As boys and girls grow into mothers, fathers, grandmas, and grandpas, their perspectives take on even more depth of gratitude, understanding, and love.
- I want to be more like my mother. Each time I am in the car with my three kids, trying to curb disagreements between my

two boys and gauge feeding times with drop off to kindergarten and my Church calling, I say to myself, "How did Mom do it with twice as many of us?" She was definitely a super mom!

My wife is one of those people. We are now in the twilight of our lives. She's been my sweetheart now for decades, and to me, she is even more beautiful than the day we were married. We've grown together to a point we are like a couple of yoked oxen, knowing when to pull and when to let up. We seem to know when the other is hungry, sleepy, or needs to go for a ride. I dread the probability that one of us will have to linger on when it's time for the other to go. It's hardly possible to think of life without her.

Now I'm a bishop and a father of five. My professional pursuits are taxing. Being a great dad is important to me, and working with others who have problems demands so much. It's often overwhelming. My bride of twenty years and my mother of forty are the stabilizing influences in my life that keep me grounded, humble, and balanced. My wife gives understanding suggestions and my mother heaps on compliments and affirmations in moments when I need them to keep me going.

I love watching my daughters and sons. They are marvelous women and men, parents and leaders. In years past I remember many days when I wondered if I was enough to be an adequate mother. Heavenly Father surely touched our efforts with His hand and made them enough. When I see them in their adult roles, I feel so thankful—constantly prayerful.

I've made a lot of bad choices in my life. I didn't walk the path my parents wanted me to. I came to see I needed to change and am currently in process. There are many things I cannot fix, and others will take a lifetime to improve. Both Mom and Dad are great. Mother, with her instinctive love and constant support, is one anchor that will help me arrive at a better place.

Sisters, daughters, mothers, grandmas—each the offspring of Eve and heavenly parentage—are among the greatest blessings of our lives. It never takes long for hearts to swell and emotions to gather when we ponder the impact of women in our lives. Bless us to appreciate them. May they know and remember their importance in our lives.

## Self-Examination for Greater Gratitude

1. Who are the women in your life? Have you thanked them often enough? When will you express appreciation to them in the future? How will you do it?
2. Make a list of reasons why you are thankful for your sister, mother, or grandmother. Record them in your journal. Consider sending them a copy telling them you'd like to share how you feel about them.
3. As a sister, mother, or grandmother, have you felt the need to improve your efforts to be better? What can you do today to show you are trying harder?

## Scriptures for Consideration and Marking

Luke 2:19
1 Timothy 4:4
D&C 46:32
Alma 57:21

## Parting Thought

I will close with an additional teaching from Elder Ballard. He invites, "Let us remember that 'the family is central to the Creator's plan for the eternal destiny of His children.' The scriptures and the teachings of the prophets and apostles help all family members to prepare together now to be together through all eternity. I pray that God will continually bless the women of the Church to find joy and happiness in their sacred roles as daughters of God" (ibid.).

# 30

# *Gratitude for Grace*

"Looking forward with an eternal perspective gives one hope, a reason to look up and feel gratitude for even the smallest bit of light." (Sister Rosemary M. Wixom, quoted in Sarah Jane Weaver, "Women's General Auxiliary Leaders Speak about Grace," *Church News*, 25 May 2014)

As a young boy I would go with my dad and brothers to fly-fish the rivers of Southwest Colorado. On occasion if the fishing wasn't great, we'd go for a hike. Sometimes we'd hike up the mountain and find a place where we could get a view from the elevated perspective of several hundred feet above the valley floor. There we could see the relationship between the main river, its tributaries, the beaver ponds, and even the lake in the distance. The elevated perspective provided insight and understanding we could not get when we were walking up a river, focused on the sport of catching and landing a brookie or rainbow trout.

Have you ever considered what it would be like to have a helicopter view of a few hundred years or even a satellite view from the beginning to the present? I wonder what it would be like for Abraham, Isaac, Jacob, and Joseph to counsel us today with their perspectives of a few thousand years. What would they say to us in the twenty-first century, and what counsel would they give? I can imagine they would be cheering us on, reminding us we are the children of the covenant. Perhaps they would say something like, "You can do it! You are the gatherers of our scattered family. You are doing so awesome. Keep it up! Keep your eyes on the task at hand, open your mouth, and bring those cousins to Jehovah, even Jesus Christ. Carry on to the end."

I wonder what Nephi would counsel us from a perspective of seeing from his day in 600 BC until now. I wonder if he wouldn't encourage us by saying, "Hang in there and be obedient in all things. I learned and have seen it over and over again through the 2,600 years of history: for the obedient, God prepares a way to accomplish what He promises. Keep it up! Keep going! Don't get tired or fatigued. You can do it!"

What would Mormon and Moroni say to us? Their perspectives would be most helpful because God permitted them to see our day, from about 1,600 or 1,700 years ago. I'll bet they would cheer us on as well. "We saw how the pride of the Nephites took us down. You're doing pretty well. Keep it up. Keep fighting that universal sin and the want for more. You have our bad example to the end that you can be wiser than we have been. We know you will make it. We've seen that part too. You can make it. Keep it up!"

What would Martin Luther and the other Reformers say to us? I wonder if they wouldn't cheer us on with extraordinary praise. Perhaps they'd say, "We protested the fact that there was an Apostasy from the time of Diocletian and Constantine and through the dark ages. We didn't fully understand it then, but we can see now that by following the Holy Spirit, giving up our lives, and being tortured and burned at the stake, the Lord was preparing for the days of Restoration, in which you are blessed to live. Come on, you've done a wonderful job. Keep it going!"

It would be interesting to hear the Deists like Thomas Jefferson and others chime with shouts of, "Carry on. We waited for the foretold Restoration, for apostles and prophets, and now you have it all. You are living our dream! Listen to the prophets and follow them. They will get you through tough spots."

How about Joseph and Hyrum, or the first missionary, Samuel Smith? What would they be saying? They would be excited to note that from those six members on April 6, 1830, we have become 15 million today. Samuel would say with excitement that when he left that day for his first mission with a backpack containing several copies of the Book of Mormon, he hadn't fathomed there would be 80,000 with a cumulative total of over a million in the last nearly 190 years.

Can you imagine a chorus of pioneer Saints—some who made it, and many who never lived to see the Great Salt Lake Basin—encouraging us to remain faithful and take advantage of our temple: "Wow. You've gone from our Kirtland and Nauvoo temples to nearly a 150 operating temples around the world. We knew it would fill the earth, but to imagine stakes, wards, and branches in nearly every nation on earth is so exciting!"

Can you hear them cheering, encouraging, and reminding us of the miracles that got them through the muddy roads of Iowa, the dusty trails, and frozen ground? They are counting on us to carry on and remain faithful until our journey's end. Can you hear them? They made it and would surely urge and inspire us to always remember that we will be enabled by grace to meet our trials in the same way it helped ease their burdens and made their challenges bearable.

Sister Jean A. Stevens of the Primary general presidency taught, "It is only with the grace of God that we can hope to contribute our part in His divine work. This grace from God gives us . . . His enabling power to do more and be more than we are on our own" (Jean A. Stevens, quoted in Sarah Jane Weaver, "Women's General Auxiliary Leaders Speak about Grace," *Church News*, 25 May 2014).

With great appreciation and gratitude that they were able to do their part, it is not hard to imagine the throngs of Saints and other good people who have preceded us, anticipating and counting on us to do our part. They know about tough times. They know that by trusting Heavenly Father and enduring to the end with willing, believing, and thankful hearts, we can do our part too. Sister Bonnie Oscarson taught, "We can look back on our long period of trial with assurance that the Lord was in charge of the plan and that He walked the path of longing, disappointment, pain, patience, and ultimately joy with us. His grace was sufficient" (Bonnie Oscarson, quoted in Sarah Jane Weaver, "Women's General Auxiliary Leaders Speak about Grace," *Church News*, 25 May 2014).

### Self-Examination for Greater Gratitude

1. How do you feel about your time on the "playing field"? Your turn on earth? What will it take to step up your level of contribution?
2. As you imagine the former and latter-day Saints on the other side of the veil cheering you on, do you feel deserving? What will you do to proceed as valiantly as they did?
3. Is there a journal entry here that ought to be written? Do it.

### Scriptures for Consideration and Marking

Jacob 6:12
Alma 7:23
D&C 97:13
Revelations 11:17
Mormon 9:31

### Parting Thought

I haven't always enjoyed funerals. Maybe it's because I'm getting closer to having my own, but I have come to appreciate Mormon funerals more and more with each passing year. For the most part, each one is a testimony that things work out in the end. From the beginning at birth—with all the ups and downs, joys and challenges, success and enduring—it all fits the Father's plan. The overview of a life helps us celebrate in an eternal perspective. May it also give us, as Sister Wixom began this chapter, "a reason to look up and feel gratitude for even the smallest bit of light."

# 31

# Paint It on Your Heart

"If you're not a full-time missionary with a missionary badge pinned on your coat, now is the time to paint one on your heart—painted, as Paul said, "not with ink, but with the Spirit of the living God." And returned missionaries, find your old missionary tag. Don't wear it, but put it where you can see it. The Lord needs you now more than ever to be an instrument in His hands. All of us have a contribution to make to this miracle." (Neil L. Andersen, "It's a Miracle," *Ensign*, May 2013)

I confess that I hope every worthy young man and woman will be able to serve a full-time mission. I understand it is not possible or in some cases even advisable. I am in complete agreement that some should be honorably excused from full-time missionary service. However, as I remember my own mission, my heart is filled with gratitude for the opportunity to live and act as an authorized servant of the Lord in Mexico. No young man was more blessed than I was to serve. My mission took my life to a whole new level. I'm sure I'm not the only one who feels that way. Those who embrace the call to serve with all their heart, might, mind, and strength will be blessed to feel the same.

I hope returned missionaries will always maintain in their minds a fondness and love for their missionary experience. Being authorized to wear His name on our chests and become His hands, feet, eyes, and voice can be an experience that should be remembered, revered, and repeated. A mission experience should be on the top of the list of things we are most grateful for in our lives.

I'm honored to have served with nearly 2,500 missionaries in Chile and Guatemala. I have seen how the process of teaching and converting good people across the earth also brings a significant change in the hearts and lives of the messengers—our missionaries. That being said, it needs to be clear that one does not have to serve a full-time mission to be righteous and inherit the blessings of the celestial kingdom or to have a wonderful life. Ecclesiastical leaders, parents, and individuals must work together for the best good of all. All of us, with or without a mission experience, can and must choose to become worthy to receive temple blessings and live a wonderful life of discipleship.

As I read and glean from Elder Andersen's quote and message, it strikes me that there is a clarion call to all members—whether we've served full-time missions or not—to become disciples of Christ and share the gospel with all of Heavenly Father's children. We are so blessed! We have the benefit of understanding the purpose of life, together with priesthood authority. We also have the charge to gather scattered Israel and to bring covenant blessings to those prepared to receive them.

We have responsibility, and therefore we will also be held accountable. As we look at Heavenly Father's children across this planet, we can see so much goodness in most of Father's children. In his first apostolic address to the Church, Elder Andersen taught, "We are not alone in praying to our Heavenly Father or in receiving answers to our prayers; our Father loves all of His children. We are not alone in sacrificing for a greater cause; there are others who are unselfish. Others share our faith in Christ. There are loyal and decent fathers and mothers in every land who love each other and love their children. There is much we can learn from the good people all around us" (Neil L. Andersen, "Come unto Him," *Ensign*, May 2009).

Our gratitude and thankfulness for our blessings compel us in serving missions and always being full-time member missionaries. We have restored truth. Elder Andersen continued in that inaugural address,

> Yet we must not shrink from what is uniquely and singularly found in The Church of Jesus Christ of Latter-day Saints. . . . Our knowledge of the divine mission of the Church should not bring feelings of superiority or arrogance but should take us to our knees, pleading for the Lord's help that we might be what we should be. But in humility we need not be timid in remembering the Lord's words: 'This is my church, and I will establish it; and nothing shall overthrow it.' Above all, we proclaim our Savior and Redeemer, Jesus Christ. All that we are—all that we will ever be—we owe to Him. (Ibid.)

We are so blessed! We have truth and authority, and tools to share the gospel with others. We don't need to and shouldn't be preachy or engage in debate or contention over our beliefs. But we can share. We can show our gratitude for the blessing of the Internet and social media to spread the message of the gospel across the planet.

In a most moving and inviting talk during BYU Education Week in 2014, Elder David A. Bednar called upon all to embrace and harness the power of the Internet to sweep the earth as with a flood of messages of the gospel. Using the power of social media enables us to reach a billion people with positive, non-preachy, and effective messages of truth. Elder Bednar invited, "Imagine the impact we can have as hundreds of thousands and millions of members of the Lord's restored Church contribute in seemingly small ways to the rising floodwaters. May our many small, individual efforts produce a steady rainfall of righteousness and truth that gradually swells a multitude of streams and rivers—and ultimately becomes a flood that sweeps the earth" (David A. Bednar,

"To Sweep the Earth as with a Flood," BYU Campus Education Week, August 19, 2014).

Never before have we been able to use such tools to share our message and blessings. Blogs, videos, email, smartphones, and all sorts of media tools make it easy for us to authentically, consistently, and effectively edify and uplift.

Elder Bednar invited, "My beloved brothers and sisters, what has been accomplished thus far in this dispensation communicating gospel messages through social media channels is a good beginning—but only a small trickle. I now extend to you the invitation to help transform the trickle into a flood. Beginning at this place on this day, I exhort you to sweep the earth with messages filled with righteousness and truth—messages that are authentic, edifying, and praiseworthy—and literally to sweep the earth as with a flood" (Ibid.).

Let us first be filled with gratitude for the blessing of the restored gospel and then with thankful hearts share the gospel by example, love, and using the tools the Lord has provided us to share it. This is truly one of the greatest and most blessed seasons of the earth's history. May we seize the day! Latch on to this opportunity to be participants. Let us paint a figurative missionary badge on your hearts and do all we can do to share the good news at every opportunity.

**Self-Examination for Greater Gratitude**

1. Write in your journal your feelings of gratitude and thankfulness for your blessings. If you've served a full-time mission, write about it. Consider all the blessings available to you.
2. Would you consider yourself actively involved in sharing the message of the gospel with others? What would it take to light the fire to do so?
3. Do you have social media accounts? If not, start there. If you are

intimidated by technology, ask your bishop if he could send one of the youth in the ward to teach you how to use it.

## Scriptures for Consideration and Marking

Daniel 2:34–35
1 Timothy 4:12
2 Corinthians 4:15
Matthew 5:16
Matthew 26:27

## Parting Thought

In his conference address, Elder Andersen concludes, "We are all in this together. With fellow ward members and missionaries, we plan and pray and help one another. Please keep the full-time missionaries in your thoughts and prayers. Trust them with your family and friends. The Lord trusts them and has called them to teach and bless those who seek Him" (Neil L. Andersen, "It's a Miracle," *Ensign*, May 2013).

# About the Author

DAVID A. Christensen's love for present-day prophets was sparked as a young returned missionary student at Brigham Young University when he took the religion class "Teachings of the Living Prophets." He has a testimony of listening to and seeking to follow those who are charged with helping us understand the Lord's will and direction in our lives. David has taught the same course, "Teaching of the Living Prophets," for over two decades at BYU–I. He sought to pass on that same testimony and love for the counsel given by living prophets to missionaries when he presided over the Chile Santiago North Mission, the Guatemala MTC, and in his service as stake president and bishop.

He counts his eight children and growing number of grandchildren as his most important converts, and his best friend and wife, Deena Bond Christensen, his eternal companion.

0 26575 16744 3